OXFORD
preparation course
for the TOEIC® test

TOEIC® IS A REGISTERED TRADEMARK OF EDUCATIONAL TESTING SERVICE (ETS).
THIS PUBLICATION IS NOT ENDORSED OR APPROVED BY ETS.

OXFORD
UNIVERSITY PRESS

OXFORD
UNIVERSITY PRESS

Great Clarendon Street, Oxford OX2 6DP

Oxford University Press is a department of the University of Oxford.
It furthers the University's objective of excellence in research, scholarship,
and education by publishing worldwide in

Oxford New York

Auckland Cape Town Dar es Salaam Hong Kong Karachi
Kuala Lumpur Madrid Melbourne Mexico City Nairobi
New Delhi Shanghai Taipei Toronto

With offices in

Argentina Austria Brazil Chile Czech Republic France Greece
Guatemala Hungary Italy Japan Poland Portugal Singapore
South Korea Switzerland Thailand Turkey Ukraine Vietnam

OXFORD and OXFORD ENGLISH are registered trade marks of
Oxford University Press in the UK and in certain other countries

ISBN: 978 0 19 456400 7

Typeset by Oxford University Press
in ITC Franklin Gothic and Monotype Calisto

Printed in China

This book is printed on paper from certified and well-managed sources.

Access to free TOEIC® practice test extract at
www.oxfordenglishtesting.com/unlock
Unlock Code: 5e7b04-884699-cc758c-42b663

ACKNOWLEDGEMENTS

The author and publisher would like to thank the following for their kind
permission to reproduce photographs and other artwork copyright
material:

Cover:
Corbis UK Ltd. (woman with laptop, architecture, couple with headphones)
Alamy (Olympic bridge)

Corbis UK Ltd. pp 9 (woman filing), 51 (measuring a window), 71 (aeroplanes
in hanger), 92 (steel construction, windmills); Digital Vision pp 28 (business
meeting), 29 (television conference); The Image Bank pp 30 (office
scene/Henry Sims), 49 (couple with architect/Donata Pizzi), 51 (house
painters/Steve Dunwell Photography), 70 (aeroplane meal/Tom Hussey),
93 (computer/Dag Sundberg); Powerstock pp 91 (biologist), 93 (watch-
maker/Zefa-Abril); Photodisc pp 7 (business meeting), 8 (woman at counter,
photocopier room), 9 (women shaking hands, man and computer),
28 (computer), 30 (business meeting), 49 (house for sale), 50 (house
construction), 51 (carpet installer), 71 (passengers on platform), 72 (ocean
liner, teenagers in diner); Robert Harding Picture Library pp 9 (man with
graphs), 29 (stock exchange), 91 (control panel/Tom Carroll/Phototake NYC);
Stone pp 7 (man writing/Bruce Ayres), 30 (business seminar/Michael
Rosenfeld, business meeting/Tim Macpherson), 50 (construction workers),
51 (Japanese sign/Andy Sacks), 70 (captain on bridge/Christian Lagereek),
72 (airline check-in/Klaus Lahnstein), 93 (clearing rubble/Chip Porter,
students in television studio/Andy Sacks); Telegraph Colour Library p 72
(man riding on a bus/Rob Brimson).

The publisher would like to thank the following individuals and
institutions for their help with reviewing and piloting material in this
course:

Ms. Rena Yoshida, Obirin University, Kanagawa; Ms. Toshie Agawa, Keisen
University, Tokyo; Ms. Chiseko Kuroda, Tsuda Jukukai Institute, Tokyo;
Mr. Nobuo Tsuda, Konan University, Hyogo; AIT Foreign Language Center,
Tokyo; Tsuda Jukukai Institute, Tokyo; Dr. Kim Hekyung, Ph.D., Department
of English, Dongseo University, Busan, Korea; Ms. Yang Soh Jeong, Korea
University, Seoul; Ms. Seo Jeong-wha, Lee Ik Hoon Language Institute,
Jongno, Seoul; Ms. Lee Kyung-hee, BCM Mokdong, Seoul; Ms. Won Jeong
Soe, PAGODA Jongno, Seoul; Ms. Kim Yul Hee, YBM E4U Jongno, Seoul;
Mr. LEE Ji-ho, TESTwise SISA, Jongno, Seoul

Contents

Introduction

The TOEIC® Test

1 What is the TOEIC test?

The Test of English for International Communication (TOEIC) was first developed in 1979 by ETS to assess the English language skills of people working in multinational companies, schools, and government organizations around the world. Since English is one of the most commonly used languages for international commerce, employers saw the need to have a common measure of the language skills of their employees and prospective employees. The new TOEIC test has evolved to take into account current theories of language proficiency and to reflect the needs of today's test users. It includes a variety of tasks and emphasizes communication.

2 Who takes the TOEIC test?

Your employer may ask you for a TOEIC score for promotion or you may have to provide a TOEIC score in order to apply for a certain job. Maybe you are finishing a language program and want to have an official score and certificate to take with you to show your employer, school, family, or friends. Whatever your reason, your TOEIC score is recognized around the world.

3 What is the format of the TOEIC test?

The TOEIC test takes two hours. It tests your listening and reading skills through a range of authentic tasks. These tasks are designed to reflect the kinds of situations you might encounter in the global business world.

Listening Test (45 minutes)	
Part 1: Photos	10 items
Part 2: Question–Response	30 items
Part 3: Conversations	30 items
Part 4: Talks	30 items
Total	100 items

Reading Test (75 minutes)	
Part 5: Incomplete Sentences	40 items
Part 6: Cloze Passages	12 items
Part 7: Reading Comprehension	48 items
Total	100 items

4 What is being tested?

Listening Test

This part tests your ability to understand spoken English. The listening items become increasingly longer and more difficult as the test proceeds, moving from one spoken sentence in Part 1 to a short talk in Part 4. You will hear varied accents, including US, British, Australian, and Canadian, in order to reflect the reality of the workplace.

In Part 1 you will see a picture in your test book and hear four short statements. You should select the statement that best describes the picture.

In Part 2 you will hear two speakers. The first speaker will ask a question or make a statement. The second speaker will give three possible responses. You should choose the best response to the question or statement.

In Part 3 you will hear some conversations between two people. You will read three questions in your test book about each conversation. Each question is followed by four responses. You should select the best response in each case.

In Part 4 you will hear some short talks by a single speaker. You will read three questions in your test book about each talk. Each question is followed by four responses. You should select the best response in each case.

Reading Test

In the Reading Test you are tested on your ability to understand written English. Your knowledge of vocabulary and grammar is tested, as well as your ability to identify the main idea of a reading passage and find the answers to questions about details.

In Part 5 you will read some incomplete sentences. Four answer choices with words or phrases are provided for each sentence. You should select the answer choice that best completes the sentence.

In Part 6 you will read a cloze passage. This is a passage with a word or phrase missing in some of the sentences. Four answer choices are provided and you should select the answer choice that best completes the sentence. You may have to refer to other parts of the passage to complete the sentence.

In Part 7 you will read a selection of texts, such as letters, articles, notices, emails, and advertisements. Each text is followed by several questions. You should select the best response to each question. In this part of the test, some reading tasks require you to read two related texts and answer questions about them. You will need to connect information from both texts to be able to answer some of the questions.

5 How do the distractors distract?

In each question of the TOEIC test, you will find what we call "distractors" among the answer choices. These answer choices seem as if they might be correct, but they are used to distract or confuse you. Some of the most common distractors in the Listening Test are:

- similar sounding words (example: *president* is spoken, *precedent* is given in the answer choices)
- reasonable answers but in the wrong context or situation (example: you see a picture of a plate on a table and an answer choice indicates that the plate is being washed)
- irrelevant answer choices (example: you see a picture of a person buying a computer and an answer choice indicates that the person is buying a camera)
- a word from the question, conversation, or talk is repeated in an answer choice (example: *president* is in the question and is also in an answer choice, but it is not the correct answer in the context)
- an illogical response (example: the question asks *what* and an answer choice indicates *where*).

In both the Listening and Reading sections of the test, you will find distractors that:

- repeat a word or make a connection with a word or phrase (example: a passage mentions architecture in San Francisco and an answer choice repeats San Francisco or includes California).
- are reasonable if a key section is misunderstood (example: you hear or read about an employee being honored and an answer choice indicates a birthday party).

Here is some advice to help you avoid choosing attractive distractors:

- read or listen to the question carefully and make sure the response actually answers the question
- read all the answer choices carefully
- identify key words that are particular to certain contexts
- think of words that could be associated with these key words
- ask yourself questions as you listen or read: where is this taking place? who is involved? what is happening?
- become familiar with parts of speech and word families.

6 Directions for the TOEIC test

The directions for each part of the TOEIC test are always the same. Become familiar with the directions so that when you take the official test you don't need to spend time reading the directions.

7 Score reports

Your performance on the TOEIC test provides the evidence for a score report. Proficiency descriptors describe in detail your abilities in listening and reading. This provides invaluable feedback which makes the test results more meaningful for you and anyone who needs to use them.

8 More information

You can get more information about the TOEIC test, test dates, and TOEIC worldwide representatives on the TOEIC website at

http://www.toeic.com

Oxford Preparation Course for the TOEIC® test

1   What is included in this course?

Practice Tests

There are two practice tests for the TOEIC test, including two audio CDs. Each test contains 200 items and provides complete practice of the actual test.

You can use the practice tests in two ways:

1   Take as much time as you need to complete the test.

2   Take the test under test conditions. Allow yourself 45 minutes for the Listening Test and 75 minutes for the Reading Test and do not use any aids (a dictionary, for example). It would be a good idea to do at least one of the tests in this way.

Each test booklet contains a full tapescript for the Listening Test. If you have difficulty in understanding the listening sections, listen and follow the tapescripts to accustom yourself to the type of spoken English you will hear in the TOEIC test.

Each test booklet also contains a detailed answer key, with explanations for each answer choice. Study the explanations provided so that you can find out why one choice is correct and the others are incorrect. One of the best ways to improve your score on the TOEIC test is to study and learn from your mistakes, and the answer key will help you to do that.

Sample answer sheets are also supplied to give you practice in using them.

Once you've checked your answers against the answer key, use the conversion table at the back of the test booklet to see your approximate TOEIC score. The table allows you to convert the number of correctly answered questions into a TOEIC score. This score is only an approximate guide and cannot be substituted for an actual TOEIC score. Make a note of the questions that were difficult for you. When you study the Student's Book, pay attention to those particular types of question, as these are the areas you should study carefully.

Student's Book

There are five chapters in the Student's Book. Together they cover the main topic areas usually found in the TOEIC test – offices and personnel, general business and finance, housing and property, travel, and technical areas. They will help you to develop the skills, strategies, and vocabulary that are necessary to do well on the test.

Each chapter is divided into the seven parts of the TOEIC listening and reading tests. Each part contains strategies and tasks to make you aware of the requirements of the test and highlights the potential traps and distractors that are used in the TOEIC test. Each part ends with a review that has test questions just like those on the TOEIC test.

The chapters in the Student's Book do not have to be studied in any order. You can pick those that you think you will need the most.

Tapescripts and answer key

The tapescripts and answer key for the Student's Book are supplied in a separate book.

2   How should I use this material?

Pick out the chapters or the parts of chapters of the Student's Book that are of interest to you and study them. Pay attention to the strategies that are presented. The strategies focus your attention on the different kinds of questions that may appear on the test and on techniques for answering the questions quickly and effectively. Work through the tasks, which are designed to improve your vocabulary and increase your level of English. These tasks may be different from the actual test questions but they are designed to improve the skills you will need to answer the questions correctly. The strategies and tasks will also help you identify the potential traps and distractors in the TOEIC test. It is important to remember these traps and be aware of them as you are taking the test.

3   What if I don't have time to do it all?

The Student's Book has been written with this in mind. It is an easy book to dip into and out of. You can focus on those parts of the test that you need to study, and leave the sections that you don't have time for. Alternatively, if there is a topic area that you need to improve on, you may focus on that chapter. By doing so, you can improve your vocabulary in that particular area.

4   Grammar Glossary

The Grammar Glossary has been included in the Student's Book to help you to better understand the strategies and tasks. Grammar terminology is sometimes used in explaining a strategy. A cross-reference to the Grammar Glossary indicates where you will find a brief explanation of the particular language point. If you feel you need to practice an area of grammar further, it is advisable to use a grammar reference book.

Chapter 1 Offices and Personnel

Listening PART 1

Strategy A

Use the pictures to identify an event.
Ask yourself *what* is taking place and *where* it is taking place.

| What? | The group is having a meeting. | What? | The man is filling out a form. |
| Where? | They are sitting around a table. | Where? | He's standing at a counter. |

Task A

Identify an event

Cross out the words or phrases that do NOT describe the event listed.

1 interview asking questions, inviting the public, answering, trying to impress, turning up the heat, giving background information

2 recruiting fair networking, applicants, trusted employee, presentation of new products, résumé, social event

3 office tour department locations, cafeteria, sightseeing, supply catalog, parking facilities, off-site drilling

4 training new employees, human resource regulations, public transportation, rating, mandatory, autonomy

5 promotion honor, bad track record, praise, special sale, raise, extra inventory

Strategy B

Be aware of prepositions of location. The TOEIC® test often uses prepositions of location (*in*, *on*, *under*, *beneath*, etc.) with words found in the picture. These prepositions could also be used with words associated with the context of the picture, but in different locations.

Compare the statements below that identify the correct location with the other options.

(A)   She's resting *at* her desk.
(B)   She's standing *by* the fountain.
(C)   She's working *behind* the counter.
(D)   She's taking flowers *from* the shelves.

The correct answer is (C).

(A)   She's ordering more paper *from* the store.
(B)   She's standing *by* the copy machine.
(C)   She's adding more pages *to* the report.
(D)   She's waiting *next to* the door.

The correct answer is (B).

> **Grammar Glossary Prepositions of Location (p116)**

Task B 🎧

Identify the location

Listen to the sentences. Check the letter that uses a preposition to describe where something is located.

6   (A) ....✓......
   (B) ....

7   (A) ....
   (B) ....

8   (A) ....
   (B) ....

9   (A) ....
   (B) ....

10 (A) ....
   (B) ....

Review 🎧

Directions: Listen and select the one statement that best describes what you see in the picture.

11

12

13

14

Listening

Part 1				
11	Ⓐ	Ⓑ	Ⓒ	Ⓓ
12	Ⓐ	Ⓑ	Ⓒ	Ⓓ
13	Ⓐ	Ⓑ	Ⓒ	Ⓓ
14	Ⓐ	Ⓑ	Ⓒ	Ⓓ

PART 2

Task A

Identify characteristics

Cross out the answer choices that do NOT answer the question. Underline the adjectives and descriptive phrases in the answer choices.

1   How was the interview with the candidate for the director's job?

   (A)   A little rough at first, and then it improved.
   (B)   The director is very well respected.
   (C)   I can't believe how well we got along.

2   What are you trying to accomplish in the training?

   (A)   Everything was finished by 10:00 a.m.
   (B)   The trainees should leave with a clear idea of the company's mission.
   (C)   Her accomplishments are too many to list.

3   An effective memo should be easy to read.

   (A)   I agree. It should be short and concise.
   (B)   He responded to it immediately.
   (C)   A good speaker.

4   What did you include in the job advertisement?

   (A)   The minimum requirements were clearly stated.
   (B)   We received over 200 responses.
   (C)   Everything except for the salary.

5   How do they decide if someone is granted a leave of absence?

   (A)   A valid reason is the top priority.
   (B)   It isn't even considered if you haven't been with the company for over a year.
   (C)   We will truly miss them around the office.

6   She's an excellent speaker because she really knows her subject.

   (A)   Also she speaks clearly and enthusiastically.
   (B)   She receives over five requests a week.
   (C)   And she truly understands her audience.

7   How are the two committees different?

   (A)   They will both meet tomorrow at 3:00.
   (B)   One is very well organized.
   (C)   Dave's meetings last more than three hours.

8   What is the annual company party like?

   (A)   Every year they renew the contract.
   (B)   Honestly, it isn't very much fun, but I feel obligated to go.
   (C)   Many employees feel that it is a good way to get to know each other.

9   How is the new database working?

   (A)   It was only installed last month.
   (B)   Every day it becomes more manageable.
   (C)   Employees are finding it very flexible.

10   How well is her replacement doing the job?

   (A)   Clients have been registering quite a few complaints.
   (B)   Extremely well, considering the challenges.
   (C)   The woman has an MBA and a law degree.

Real Spoken English
There are many ways to ask someone to describe something. *Tell me about it*, and *What's it like?* are very common. *Can you describe it?* is more formal.

Strategy B

Listen for words that tell you something happens frequently.

> He goes to the gym *every day* after work.
> She doesn't *let a day pass* without her afternoon coffee.
> They are *constantly* advertising for new managers.
> This company is *always* calling emergency meetings.

Grammar Glossary **Adverbs: Frequency Words (p112)**

Task B

Identify a frequent action

Mark the sentences that indicate a frequent event with an *F*. Mark the sentences that indicate an occasional event with an *O*. Then, underline the word or expression which gave you the answer.

11 (A) He never arrives on time. ...F......
    (B) The meetings are always longer than stated. ...F......
    (C) They occasionally meet after everyone has gone home. ...O......

12 (A) Without fail, the new employees are shocked at the amount of paperwork to be filled out. ....
    (B) Once in a while employees need to file reports. ....
    (C) What was once a monthly occurrence has now turned into a daily routine. ....

13 (A) Every day they pile on more and more responsibilities. ....
    (B) From time to time, every person in the office is expected to help. ....
    (C) All employees are required to assist at least once a month. ....

14 (A) Now that she has started, she can't stop sending out surveys. ....
    (B) You won't have to answer the questions more than a handful of times. ....
    (C) We receive the questionnaire several times a year. ....

15 (A) Part of your daily job responsibilities is to take the messages. ....
    (B) You may be asked on occasion to take messages for the president. ....
    (C) She always returns my message the same day. ....

Review 🎧

Directions: Listen and select the best response to the question or statement.

Listening

Part 2				
16	Ⓐ Ⓑ Ⓒ	21	Ⓐ Ⓑ Ⓒ	
17	Ⓐ Ⓑ Ⓒ	22	Ⓐ Ⓑ Ⓒ	
18	Ⓐ Ⓑ Ⓒ	23	Ⓐ Ⓑ Ⓒ	
19	Ⓐ Ⓑ Ⓒ	24	Ⓐ Ⓑ Ⓒ	
20	Ⓐ Ⓑ Ⓒ	25	Ⓐ Ⓑ Ⓒ	

PART 3

Strategy A

Use the questions and answers to identify a method.
A method often includes several steps and uses the simple present tense to describe something that is done repeatedly. Look for questions that begin with *how*.

How does she make decisions?
She *reads* all the information and *asks* for other opinions. Then she *considers* her goals and *makes* a decision.

Task A

Identify a method

Cross out those sentences which do NOT describe a method. Then, in the remaining sentences, underline the method.

1   How do you find the right applicant for the job?
    (A) Generally, my first step is to <u>call</u> the candidate and <u>get some information</u> from them.
    (B) ~~The candidate did not have the necessary experience.~~
    (C) ~~She was asking for too much money.~~
    (D) It's best to <u>reject</u> unqualified candidates <u>before interviewing</u> them.

2   What is your secret for running a successful meeting?
    (A) The meeting is always run by the director of the department.
    (B) They are more successful when an agenda is distributed beforehand.
    (C) He tries not to keep them more than an hour and a half.
    (D) For the first time, every single employee was present.

3   How are employee's references checked?
    (A) A background check is done for everyone.
    (B) A sales representative makes a cold call.
    (C) Brochures are sent out to the prospective client.
    (D) The office revenue was over $1.5 million.

4   How do you start to develop an advertising campaign?
    (A) After weeks of talks, they refused our terms of agreement.
    (B) Once we know who our audience is, we start to design a message.
    (C) New York advertising costs are some of the highest in the world.
    (D) We do extensive market research.

5   What is included in your background check of an employee?
    (A) All the employees' files are checked for any negative incidents.
    (B) Anyone with unsatisfactory reviews is given a warning.
    (C) The supervisor's evaluations are reviewed.
    (D) They were fired without notice.

Strategy B

Look for questions that ask to identify emotions. Pay attention to questions that begin with *how*. Read the answer choices quickly. Look for words that describe feelings.

How does the man feel?
How will the woman react?

Task B

Identify emotions

Read a line from a conversation. Then cross out the answer choices that are NOT possible.

6   "It's my first time to run the staff meeting."
    How might the woman feel?

    (A) Corrupt
    (B) Worried
    (C) Appropriate
    (D) Apprehensive

7   "Dr. Lau is retiring after 45 years of service."
    How might the speaker feel toward Dr. Lau?
    (A) Impressed
    (B) Energetic
    (C) Envious
    (D) Incensed

8   "John will receive his warning letter this afternoon."
    How might John feel?

    (A) Dubious
    (B) Defensive
    (C) Defiant
    (D) Delighted

9   "The evaluations from the training session were returned with very negative and disapproving comments."
    How did the evaluators feel about the program?

    (A) Critical
    (B) Evasive
    (C) Disgusted
    (D) Avid

Review 🎧

Directions: Listen and select the best response to each question.

10 How long does the man spend reading his email?

    (A) Ten minutes
    (B) Sixty minutes
    (C) Two hours
    (D) All day

11 How often does the woman look at her junk email folder?

    (A) Hourly
    (B) Daily
    (C) Weekly
    (D) Monthly

12 How does the man feel?

    (A) Exhausted
    (B) Relaxed
    (C) Annoyed
    (D) Amused

13 What is the man's concern about the faxes?

    (A) He sent them to the wrong person.
    (B) He misplaced them.
    (C) He forgot to send them.
    (D) He threw them in the wastebasket.

14 What does he always do with sent faxes?

    (A) Places them in a special folder
    (B) Rereads them for mistakes
    (C) Reprints them to make a copy
    (D) Puts them in the wastebasket

15 How does the man feel?

    (A) Carefree
    (B) Worn out
    (C) Worried
    (D) Pleased

Listening				
Part 3				
10	Ⓐ	Ⓑ	Ⓒ	Ⓓ
11	Ⓐ	Ⓑ	Ⓒ	Ⓓ
12	Ⓐ	Ⓑ	Ⓒ	Ⓓ
13	Ⓐ	Ⓑ	Ⓒ	Ⓓ
14	Ⓐ	Ⓑ	Ⓒ	Ⓓ
15	Ⓐ	Ⓑ	Ⓒ	Ⓓ

PART 4

Strategy A

Use the questions and answers to focus on specific dates. Look for questions that begin with *when*.

> *When* is the meeting?
> *When* will the new computers arrive?
> *When* is Mr. Lee retiring?

In the answers look for specific date markers which refer to a precise month, day or time.

Specific Date Markers

Months:	in *January, February, March, April*, etc.
Days of the week:	on *Monday, Tuesday, Wednesday, Thursday*, etc.
Time:	at *5:45 a.m*, in *19 weeks*, for *24 minutes*, etc.

Grammar Glossary Adverbs: Date/Time/Sequence Markers (p112)

Task A

Identify specific dates

Cross out the answer choices that do NOT indicate specific dates.

1.
(A) Every third Monday of the month
(B) On the following Monday at noon
(C) At 5:00 p.m. on the day that you choose
(D) Any Monday that is convenient for you

2.
(A) It ran from May 23rd through the 29th.
(B) Fourteen days is the longest trip she has taken.
(C) It lasted for around two weeks.
(D) She left for her trip on the fifth of May.

3.
(A) He'll start sometime next month.
(B) He already started working.
(C) His start date is the Tuesday after next.
(D) He gave his notice on November 2nd and will begin thirty days after.

4.
(A) Your computer will be on your desk first thing in the morning.
(B) The shipment of new computers was delayed, but they should arrive any day now.
(C) They guaranteed delivery within twenty-one days from the order date.
(D) The order arrived yesterday.

5.
(A) All evaluations are due in two weeks with no exceptions.
(B) Evaluations are always given the second Monday of February.
(C) I received my evaluation three weeks late last year.
(D) You can turn in the evaluation any time after the first of the month.

6.
(A) Mr. Schwartz is celebrating his twentieth year with the company today.
(B) Jim was promoted on the Monday after we moved into our new offices.
(C) He began work sometime in May of 1990.
(D) The office staff are planning a party tomorrow at 5:00 p.m.

Strategy B

Use the questions and answers to identify responsibilities. Look for questions that begin with *who* to identify the person who is doing something.
Look for questions that begin with *what* to identify the actions the person should do or take.

Who is responsible for hiring?
What is she responsible for doing?
Who is in charge of the meeting?
What are his job responsibilities?

Task B 🎧

Identify responsibilities

You will hear two talks. Before each talk begins, read the answer choices quickly. Then listen and choose the best answer.

7 Who must be notified first if an employee is sick?

(A) The human resource manager
(B) The supervisor
(C) Giovanni
(D) The company doctor

8 Who will contact the doctor?

(A) The employee
(B) The supervisor
(C) Mark Johnson
(D) The human resource manager

9 What is each manager expected to do?

(A) Discuss plans for the next two years
(B) Report on a region's performance
(C) Outline his or her travel agenda
(D) Organize the next meeting

10 Who is responsible for the United States?

(A) No one
(B) Everyone
(C) The first presenter
(D) The last presenter

Review 🎧

Directions: Listen and select the best response to each question.

11 When will employees start to pack their boxes?

(A) Wednesday at noon
(B) On Friday
(C) Sometime on Tuesday afternoon
(D) Before Tuesday noon

12 Who is responsible for organizing the move?

(A) Each employee
(B) The announcer
(C) Mark Chow
(D) Suzanne Green

13 What kind of boxes should be put on the storage dock?

(A) Important boxes
(B) Non-essential boxes
(C) Unpacked boxes
(D) Unlabeled boxes

---

14 What is Diana Sanchez responsible for?

(A) Reading through the package
(B) Driving the group to the meeting
(C) Determining who is in each group
(D) Doing the new employee training

15 When will the training take place?

(A) Next Friday
(B) Today
(C) Over the next three Fridays
(D) Between today and Friday

16 How many hours will they meet altogether?

(A) Three
(B) Six
(C) Nine
(D) Twelve

Listening				
Part 4				
11	Ⓐ	Ⓑ	Ⓒ	Ⓓ
12	Ⓐ	Ⓑ	Ⓒ	Ⓓ
13	Ⓐ	Ⓑ	Ⓒ	Ⓓ
14	Ⓐ	Ⓑ	Ⓒ	Ⓓ
15	Ⓐ	Ⓑ	Ⓒ	Ⓓ
16	Ⓐ	Ⓑ	Ⓒ	Ⓓ

Reading PART 5

Strategy A

Look at the sentence to identify the prepositions. Then look what follows the preposition. This is the object. A prepositional phrase is made up of a preposition and an object.

> The new employee was given a long list *(of fifteen items)* to be completed *(by the next day)*.

You see two prepositional phrases in the sentence. The prepositions are *of* and *by*. Each has an object: *fifteen items* and *the next day*.

On the TOEIC test, the incomplete part of the sentence may follow a preposition. Check carefully if it is part of a prepositional phrase. If so, the missing word will be a noun – the object of the preposition.

Grammar Glossary **Prepositions: Objects (p116)**

Task A

Identify the objects of prepositions

Mark the prepositional phrase(s) in each of the sentences by placing parentheses around the phrase. Underline the object(s) of the preposition.

1. The entire staff gathered (around <u>the computer</u>) to see the software demonstration.

2. She had only three days remaining of her vacation time, so she received no pay for the other ten days of her trip.

3. The supervisor, after serious thought, denied his employee's request for a leave of absence.

4. When the company won the contract with the government, it had to begin a policy requiring all employees with access to the building to wear identification badges.

5. Everyone in the office gave some money to purchase a farewell gift for Ms. Woo.

6. The memo was lost in a pile of papers that ended up on the secretary's desk.

Strategy B

Read the answer choices quickly to find the correct word. If you see similar prefixes or suffixes, be careful to choose the word with the correct meaning.

> The director of personnel ………. the résumés before the candidates came for an interview.
> (A) preselected
> (B) preferred
> (C) predicted
> (D) previewed

You can quickly see that the common prefix is *pre-*, meaning *before*. Read the second part of each word carefully to work out the answer.

D, *previewed* is correct. The second part of the word *viewed* meaning *looked at*, so the director *looked at* the résumés *before* the candidates came for an interview.

Grammar Glossary **Prefixes and Suffixes (p116)**

Task B

Identify the correct word

Check the word which has the same meaning as the underlined word.
Then enter the common prefix or suffix.

7   She looked through the pile of applications.

   (A)   recalled
   (B)   reviewed ✓
   (C)   reinforced
   (D)   reassessed

   Common prefix or suffix: ...re-...

8   The manager called the referee to inquire about the applicant.

   (A)   reference
   (B)   residence
   (C)   precedence
   (D)   inference

   Common prefix or suffix: ………

9   The board meeting was delayed due to members being out of the country.

   (A)   postulated
   (B)   posterior
   (C)   postmarked
   (D)   postponed

   Common prefix or suffix: ………

10   The audience thought the Korean dancers were marvellous.

   (A)   terrific
   (B)   realistic
   (C)   authentic
   (D)   ethnic

   Common prefix or suffix: ………

11   The award consisted of a trip to the Bahamas and a check for $5,000.

   (A)   included
   (B)   insisted
   (C)   incorporated
   (D)   influenced

   Common prefix or suffix: ………

Review

Directions: Select the best answer to complete the sentence.

12 With all the clutter, the customer didn't have a very favorable .... of the office.

   (A) revision
   (B) provision
   (C) impression
   (D) vision

13 All workers have the right to review the terms of their ....

   (A) employ
   (B) employment
   (C) employee
   (D) employed

14 She met with the .... firm as soon as she finished her degree.

   (A) recruitment
   (B) recruits
   (C) recruited
   (D) recruit

15 They made a mistake in not considering the .... of leasing the office furniture.

   (A) option
   (B) operating
   (C) opinion
   (D) opposition

16 The year was so .... for the company that every employee received an additional 10% bonus.

   (A) professional
   (B) prolific
   (C) proactive
   (D) profitable

Reading

Part 5				
12	Ⓐ	Ⓑ	Ⓒ	Ⓓ
13	Ⓐ	Ⓑ	Ⓒ	Ⓓ
14	Ⓐ	Ⓑ	Ⓒ	Ⓓ
15	Ⓐ	Ⓑ	Ⓒ	Ⓓ
16	Ⓐ	Ⓑ	Ⓒ	Ⓓ

PART 6

Grammar Glossary Verb Tenses (p118)

Task A

Identify the verb tenses

Underline the verbs in the sentence and write their tenses.

1   The temporary receptionist's work <u>has been</u> so impressive that the director <u>is offering</u> him a full-time job today!

present perfect, present progressive
....

2   Everyone in the office knew about the division's personnel problems, but no one wanted to tell the president.

....

3   The number of employees who are asking for flexible schedules is on the increase.

....

4   He didn't want to be disturbed, so he asked his assistant to redirect all calls during his morning meeting.

....

5   Due to the restructuring, this office will be closed and all the employees will relocate to the head office or work out of their homes.

....

Strategy B

On the TOEIC test, you may have to choose a correct pronoun. The pronoun may refer to a noun elsewhere in the passage. You may have to read before or after the sentence to complete it correctly.

> Mr. Wilson's file should have been on Melissa Green's desk, but instead ____ was found in John Baxter's filing cabinet.
>
> (A) he
> (B) she
> (C) it
> (D) they

You should determine what noun would make sense in that blank. Who or what was found – *a file, a desk, John Baxter*? The most logical choice is Mr. Wilson's *file*. You should choose (C), *it*, to complete the sentence.

Grammar Glossary Pronouns (p116)

Task B

Identify the correct form of the pronoun

Underline the correct pronouns.

6   Even though Maria has several years of marketing experience, *it / they* was with a completely different industry and we don't feel that *it / they* will help *we / us*.

7   *They / Their* offices will be closed for the holiday so you should call *he / him* back on Tuesday morning.

8   All of *he / his* preparation served *his / him* well when *he / him* began the training program.

9   The fax machine will automatically redial *she / her* number if *it / her* is busy the first try.

10   The managers want to change *it / their* company's phone system so that *it / their* customers don't have to listen to a lengthy recording.

11   Because *it / their* employees work such long hours, the executive management team have decided to construct a gym in the basement of *its / their* facilities which everyone can use.

12   In order to boost *its / they* profits, Ikon has begun Spanish language classes for executives.

13   As soon as *she / her* reached *she / her* five year mark, *she / her* turned in *she / her* letter of resignation.

14   Ms. Lu will take *you / your* through *we / our* Start Program to begin the training.

15   It was *he / his* responsibility to confirm *they / their* plans and that everything would be ready.

Review

Directions: Select the best answer to complete the text.

Questions 16–19 refer to the following email.

To: Nathalie Cuevas
From: Margy Boyd
Subject: Executive recruitment search

Dear Ms. Cuevas:

When you contracted with us to find candidates for the position of Director of Public Relations in your company, we _____ to send you a list of potential candidates for review within four weeks. However, one name keeps

16 (A) will promise
    (B) promise
    (C) have promised
    (D) promised

coming up during our search and we thought we should bring his application to your attention immediately.

Terrance Matthew is an exceptional public relations specialist who is both visionary and practical. In our discussions with _____, he demonstrated that he clearly understands the current situation with your

17 (A) him
    (B) them
    (C) it
    (D) her

company and feels he could make a significant contribution not only to building your company's PR department, but also to establishing _____ place in the city's vibrant and growing culture.

18 (A) our
    (B) their
    (C) its
    (D) your

Although he has not been in an executive leadership position, he _____ as an integral part of a

19 (A) operated
    (B) will operate
    (C) has been operated
    (D) has operated

"leadership committee" composed of the senior mangers of the company where he is now employed.

Mr. Matthew has all of the qualifications needed to head and build a department. He has a clear idea of what is involved in the position you are offering and has no reservations about his abilities to accomplish what needs to be done.

I have attached his résumé and look forward to hearing from you at your earliest convenience.

Sincerely yours,
Margy Boyd
Recruitment Specialist

Reading

Part 6

16	Ⓐ	Ⓑ	Ⓒ	Ⓓ
17	Ⓐ	Ⓑ	Ⓒ	Ⓓ
18	Ⓐ	Ⓑ	Ⓒ	Ⓓ
19	Ⓐ	Ⓑ	Ⓒ	Ⓓ

PART 7

Strategy A

Use the question and answers to focus on location.
Read the questions and answer choices before you read the passage.
Look for place markers to indicate where something is taking place.

Place Markers
Look for the following types of words to identify a place or location.
Remember that these words are usually capitalized.
Names of cities, states, countries: *Chicago, California, Canada,* etc.
Names of streets: *San Bernado Street, Golden Avenue,* etc.
Names of specific buildings, theaters: *The Eiffel Tower, King's Theater,* etc.

Where does Mr. Johns suggest holding the meeting?
(A) In Gaylor St.
(B) In Spain
(C) At his office
(D) At the Los Angeles office

Ms. Joanne Swift
Director of Human Resources
Convac Financial Services
1122 Gaylor St.
Los Angeles, CA 92710

Dear Ms. Swift:

I received your message yesterday concerning an interview time. I am very interested in meeting with you. Unfortunately, I will be in Spain on a business trip from June 30 through July 6. Would it be possible to meet at your office in Los Angeles sometime during the week of July 10?

Please contact me at your earliest convenience.

Sincerely,
Jay Johns
Jay Johns

From the question, you know to look for a location. Reading the letter quickly, you see a number of places: *Gaylor St.*, *Los Angeles* and *Spain*. Mr. Johns wrote the letter to Ms. Swift, asking specifically for an interview in Ms. Swift's Los Angeles office. The correct answer is (D).

Task A

Identify a location

Choose the answer choice that does NOT have an example of the underlined word.

1   Ms. Jones has lived in six different <u>countries</u>.
    (A) Austria has a reputation for its conservative population.
    (B) The director has only positive things to say about London.
    (C) The winters are difficult in Canada.
    (D) They closed the office in Hong Kong.

2   Our office has changed <u>streets</u>.
    (A) On the second floor of 532 Muenster
    (B) Parallel to 9 de Julio Boulevard
    (C) In Exeter
    (D) At the corner of Pine and Sarasota

3   The firm is closed for all <u>major holidays</u>.
    (A) New Year's Day is celebrated at different times by different cultures.
    (B) In some countries, the first of May, May Day, honors workers.
    (C) Christmas, Ramadan, and Passover are all marked by religious ceremonies.
    (D) The office is open only from Monday to Friday.

4   We have branches in every <u>continent</u>.
    (A) Our first one was in North America.
    (B) We have ten branches in South America.
    (C) The Pacific Rim is one area we want to expand to.
    (D) We recently opened a branch in Asia.

Strategy B

You may be asked to identify a synonym for a word in the passage. First, look at the answer choices. Try to identify the synonym without the context. Then quickly look for that word in the passage. You will be given some help to locate the word. Can you substitute the synonym for the word in the passage?

The words "sign up" in line 4 are closest in meaning to

(A) line up
(B) turn up
(C) advertise
(D) put your name on

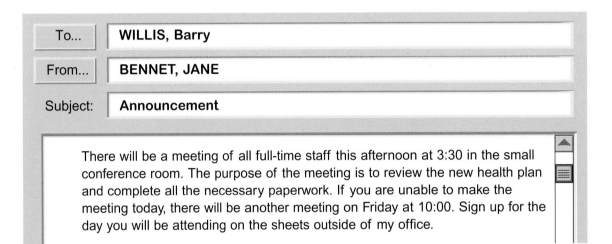

(D) is the correct answer. *Sign up* means to write your name or to register for an event. (A) *line up* could almost be substituted in the sentence. You could line up on the day you will be attending, but this verb is impossible because of the phrase *on the sheets*. (B) *Turn up*, meaning to appear on the day you will be attending, could also be substituted in the sentence, if it did not end with *on the sheets*. (C) This answer choice confuses the similar meanings of *sign* and *advertise*.

Task B

Identify the context

Match the words in italics in the statements (5–10) with the contexts (A–F).

5 She is *leaving* her job in New York.

6 They are revising the office safety *procedures*.

7 They are hiring many *multilingual* employees.

8 The meeting will be *adjourned* soon.

9 She has been working *overtime* a lot lately.

10 Four members of the board were asked to *resign*.

(A) The company needs to take precautions to avoid accidents in the workplace.

(B) We have to wait for the president to arrive.

(C) She is moving to Europe to be closer to her family.

(D) The office is understaffed so she has had to fill in for people who are sick or on vacation.

(E) It became clear that they had a conflict of interest so they had to leave.

(F) They have opened several new branches all over the world.

Strategy C

Some questions in the double passage set in the TOEIC test may require you to interpret information from both passages. You will need to understand information from both passages to answer the question correctly.

Read the questions and answer choices quickly. Can you answer the question with information from just one passage or do you need information from both passages?

One of the questions might ask for a *result*. These questions usually begin with *what*.

What will happen to the report now?

    (A) It won't be approved in time.
    (B) It won't be sent by overnight mail.
    (C) It will be sent to the shareholders on Tuesday.
    (D) It will be delivered before noon on Monday.

To:	George Gonzales
From:	Margot Chantal
Subject:	Quarterly Report
Date:	Monday, January 5

I sent the quarterly report to you this morning by overnight mail. I don't want it to get lost like last time. You should receive it no later than 10:30 a.m. tomorrow, January 6. I hope you can check the numbers in the report and approve it by tomorrow afternoon. We need to send it to the shareholders tomorrow night.

TELEPHONE CALL   **While You Were Out**

To:	*Margot*
From:	*George Gonzales*
Time:	*4:30 p.m.*
Date:	*6 January*

Message:
Snow storm delayed delivery. George will look at the report tonight and get back to you tomorrow.

The correct answer is (A). The report arrived late so George did not have time to approve it by Tuesday afternoon. (B) This option repeats words from the email, but the report has already been sent. (C) The report was to be sent to the shareholders on Tuesday, but it was not approved in time so this will not happen. (D) The report was to have been delivered before noon on Tuesday, not Monday.

Task C

Identify a result

Match the statements (11–15) with the results (A–E).

11 1 Her résumé was impressive.
     2 Other candidates were more qualified.

12 1 Company policy states that employees must be at their desks by 9:00 a.m.
     2 Mr. Wilson had no excuse for arriving every day at 10:30 a.m.

13 1 The new software program is very difficult to use.
     2 Training for the new program is not on the calendar.

14 1 Ms. Lee increased company sales by 33%.
     2 Our company rewards high performers.

15 1 We started a new promotional campaign.
     2 Our revenues exceeded projections.

(A) His employment was terminated.

(B) We extended the contract of the new advertising firm.

(C) She was not invited for an interview.

(D) Most employees don't know how to use the program.

(E) She received a bonus in her paycheck.

Review

Directions: Read the letter and select the best answer for each question.

Questions 16–20 refer to the following letter and announcement.

Valentina Saguier
Office Manager
270 Siena
Asuncion, Paraguay

Dear Ms. Saguier:

Thank you for your recent payment for your Villarica account.

We are now in receipt of payment for all of your branches, except one. Unfortunately, we still have not received payment from Branch 11. This account pays late every month, but for the past four months they have not paid at all. If we do not receive payment in full within 15 days, we will be forced to cancel this account.

We understand that you are expanding and now have stores throughout the country, with your main office located in Miami. However, we cannot overlook the amount of money that is due and the manner in which payments are made.

Please contact us immediately or send the outstanding payment to our Accounting Department here in Boston.

Sincerely,
Federico Marquez
Federico Marquez

WATCH US GROW!!

Welcome La Paz to our family

To celebrate the opening of our twelfth branch in La Paz, Bolivia, we are giving a 10% discount on all products in our stores across the Americas.

Ten years ago we had one small store in Asuncion. Now we have twelve branches:

1996	Asuncion	2001	Cordoba
1997	Villarica	2002	Cuzco
1997	São Paulo	2003	Belem
1998	Bariloche	2004	Lima
1999	Santiago	2005	Encarnacion
2000	Miami	2006	La Paz

16 Why did Mr. Marquez write the letter?

(A) To warn of pending action
(B) To thank Ms. Saguier for the payment
(C) To cancel an account in Villarica
(D) To congratulate Ms. Saguier on her expansion

17 Which branch is in arrears?

(A) Asuncion
(B) Villarica
(C) Encarnacion
(D) La Paz

18 Why does he think that it is difficult for Ms. Saguier to make the payments?

(A) Many of the stores are closing.
(B) They have stores in many different locations.
(C) She doesn't understand the business.
(D) She lives in Miami.

19 Where is Federico Marquez located?

(A) In Miami
(B) In Encarnacion
(C) In the branch in Asuncion
(D) At an office in Boston

20 The word "forced" in paragraph 2, line 4 of the letter, is closest in meaning to

(A) disappointed
(B) obliged
(C) prevented
(D) determined

Reading

Part 7				
16	Ⓐ	Ⓑ	Ⓒ	Ⓓ
17	Ⓐ	Ⓑ	Ⓒ	Ⓓ
18	Ⓐ	Ⓑ	Ⓒ	Ⓓ
19	Ⓐ	Ⓑ	Ⓒ	Ⓓ
20	Ⓐ	Ⓑ	Ⓒ	Ⓓ

Chapter 2 General Business and Finance

Listening PART 1

Strategy A

Use the pictures to guess vocabulary. Look at the pictures and list the things you see in your head. Some things you may recognize, but some things you may not be able to name specifically. For example, in the first picture, two of the people have books. You can recognize a book from its shape, but what kind of books are they? They could be appointment books, diaries, address books, instruction manuals, etc.

| What? | telephone, laptop, Post-it® Notes, sellotape, a stapler, a stamp, a computer, a chair, office workers | What? | computer screen, keyboard, mouse, mouse mat, files |
| Possible items | diaries, a folder | Possible items | floppy disks, client records |

Task A

Identify objects

Cross out the word(s) that do NOT belong in the group.

1   check book, deposit slip, library, checks, savings account, help sign

2   weights, balance sheet, debits, linens, assets, overhead costs

3   division, stock, shares, dividends, traders, common room

4   broker, manager, bands, bonds, bear market, risk

5   interest rates, rebate, loans, marketing, credit check, mortgage

Strategy B

The TOEIC® test often asks you to guess
The guess may or may not be true, but ba

Look at the picture and ask yourself wh
answer choices and compare the correct
Ask yourself what part of the wrong ar

(A) They're waiting for
technician.
(B) They're relaxing in
(C) They're participati
conference.
(D) They're watching

The correct answer is (C)

rs are in the produce

fans are cheering for their

is are voting in an election.

ers are making a trade.

er is (D).

Task B

Identify an event

The sentences in the left c ... **in the right column (A–E)**
guess what is happening. ... **n event.**

6 He is calculating numbers.
7 The woman is handing the teller some money.
8 He is giving the clerk a credit card.
9 The group is looking at some property.
10 The couple is meeting with a bank officer.

(A) ... ing for a loan.
(B) ... s preparing the budget.
(C) The real estate agent is showing the house.
(D) The tourist is buying U.S. dollars.
(E) He just purchased a stereo system.

Review 🎧

Directions: Listen and select the one statement that best describes what you see in the picture.

11

12

13

14

Listening

Part 1				
11	Ⓐ	Ⓑ	Ⓒ	Ⓓ
12	Ⓐ	Ⓑ	Ⓒ	Ⓓ
13	Ⓐ	Ⓑ	Ⓒ	Ⓓ
14	Ⓐ	Ⓑ	Ⓒ	Ⓓ

PART 2

Grammar Glossary **Conditional: should/would** (p113)

Strategy A

Listen for questions and answer choices that include suggestions. The word *should* usually indicates a suggestion.

> Who *should* she contact when she gets to Paris?
> The branch manager will be able to help her.
> She could call the branch manager.
> I would contact the branch manager.

All three of the responses give suggestions. *Should* in the question indicates that a suggestion is probably necessary. Be careful, however, not all questions that include *should* are asking for suggestions, and not all questions that ask for suggestions begin with *should*.

Task A

Identify a suggestion

Read the conversations. Cross out the question if it does NOT ask for a suggestion. Underline the suggestion given in the response.

1. **A:** Who should review the preliminary budget numbers?
    B: Peju Tyler has done a great job of analyzing the budget in the past.
2. **A:** What bank should we use to finance the expansion?
    B: Let's discuss that with our accountant.
3. **A:** Should the company be opening so many new stores at the same time?
    B The President feels that they must be aggressive now.
4. **A:** How would you use the money to improve efficiency?
    B: I would spend it on additional training for the employees.
5. **A:** With lower interest rates, should we refinance our mortgage?
    B: You won't find better rates!
6. **A:** We should finish the projections by tonight, shouldn't we?
    B: Yes, unless we run into some problems.
7. **A:** How can I lower my interest rate payments?
    B: You could pay the entire balance every month.
8. **A:** How can they increase their revenue?
    B: Have they considered spending more on advertising?
9. **A:** When should we submit our requests for next year?
    B: The deadline is November 30.
10. **A:** What should I do with the budgets from 1997 and 1998?
    B: I would keep them in the locked filing cabinets in the large conference room.

Real spoken English
Words with positive meanings like *better* may not always be positive.
It is important to read the whole sentence.

Fabio could be better with details.	*means*	Fabio is not very good with details.
Hellena Products has seen better years.	*means*	This is a very bad period for Hellena Products.

Strategy B

Listen for questions that begin with *how* to identify a method of doing something.

> *How* did he finish the research?
> *How* are the workers organized?
> *How* will the managers be advised of their budgets?

Task B

Identify a method

First, underline the object in each question (11–15). Then, match the most likely method (A–E) with the question.

11	How did he do such an excellent job on that <u>report</u>?	*B*
12	How is the company able to issue more stock?	....
13	How did they improve their credit rating?	....
14	How will they attract more investors?	....
15	How was she able to make so much money in the stock market?	....

(A)   They are counting on word of mouth.
(B)   He compiled input from all of his colleagues.
(C)   Her friends think that it was all a matter of luck.
(D)   The company collected on its outstanding accounts.
(E)   There are still available shares from the initial offering.

Review 🎧

Directions: Listen and select the best response to the question or statement.

Listening

Part 2

16	Ⓐ	Ⓑ	Ⓒ
17	Ⓐ	Ⓑ	Ⓒ
18	Ⓐ	Ⓑ	Ⓒ
19	Ⓐ	Ⓑ	Ⓒ
20	Ⓐ	Ⓑ	Ⓒ
21	Ⓐ	Ⓑ	Ⓒ
22	Ⓐ	Ⓑ	Ⓒ
23	Ⓐ	Ⓑ	Ⓒ
24	Ⓐ	Ⓑ	Ⓒ
25	Ⓐ	Ⓑ	Ⓒ

PART 3

Task A

Identify the performance level

Read the sentences. Underline the part of the sentence that describes the performance level. Then put the sentences in order from best to worst (1=best and 3=worst).

1. (A) Luca is doing <u>well</u> for a <u>beginner</u>. ....2....
   (B) Enzo is amazing at the job. ....
   (C) Fabio could be better with details and customer relations. ....

2. (A) Athens Food has improved considerably. ....
   (B) Hellena Products has seen better years. ....
   (C) Mykonos Desserts is having a record year. ....

3. (A) Our current economic situation can't get any worse. ....
   (B) Our revenues for fiscal year 2003 should exceed expectations. ....
   (C) The situation is beginning to look up in our Eastern markets. ....

4. (A) His investment portfolio has taken a downward turn. ....
   (B) Stock prices have been steadily climbing. ....
   (C) Her investment has tripled in value. ....

5. (A) Due to his exceptional performance he will receive a raise. ....
   (B) The marketing department is scaling back its projects. ....
   (C) As of next month, the service department will be permanently closed. ....

Strategy B

Look for questions that ask you for characteristics about a specific thing or person.

What are the requirements for the job?
How does their benefits package compare to others?
What does the speaker say about the software program?

Task B

Identify characteristics

Cross out the answer choices that do NOT identify specific characteristics.
Then underline the words or phrases in the sentences that do identify characteristics.

6   What does the speaker say the budget process is like?

    (A) It's long and time consuming.
    (B) It's stressful.
    (C) It takes place at the same time each year.
    (D) It's headed by the senior financial analyst.

7   How do stock dividends work?

    (A) They are distributed quarterly.
    (B) They are based on company earnings.
    (C) They were sent by mistake.
    (D) They will be canceled this year.

8   What is a down payment?

    (A) It's necessary to purchase a home.
    (B) It's traditionally 20% of the total price.
    (C) It was rejected by the bank.
    (D) It shows intention to pay.

9   What does the speaker say about the loan the partners applied for?

    (A) It will be paid over a 10-year period.
    (B) It can be paid in full before its maturity date.
    (C) It was needed to build the new office.
    (D) It requires a lot of paperwork.

Review 🎧

Directions: Listen and select the best response to each question.

10 Who was the memo addressed to?

    (A) Management
    (B) The women's department
    (C) Travel agents
    (D) The finance department

11 What kind of hotels do they use?

    (A) Luxury
    (B) 4-star
    (C) Resorts
    (D) Inexpensive

12 What does one speaker suggest they do?

    (A) Stop traveling
    (B) Eat at fancy restaurants
    (C) Take a bus home
    (D) Work at the office

---

13 What does the man think about the financial report?

    (A) He hasn't received the report yet.
    (B) The information was correct.
    (C) On close examination, it was fine.
    (D) The numbers were too high.

14 What was the woman's opinion?

    (A) She thought it was carelessly done.
    (B) She thought everything was alright.
    (C) She wasn't satisfied with the information.
    (D) She couldn't justify the numbers.

15 How did the shareholders receive the last report?

    (A) Critically
    (B) Happily
    (C) Appreciatively
    (D) Favorably

Listening

Part 3				
10	Ⓐ	Ⓑ	Ⓒ	Ⓓ
11	Ⓐ	Ⓑ	Ⓒ	Ⓓ
12	Ⓐ	Ⓑ	Ⓒ	Ⓓ
13	Ⓐ	Ⓑ	Ⓒ	Ⓓ
14	Ⓐ	Ⓑ	Ⓒ	Ⓓ
15	Ⓐ	Ⓑ	Ⓒ	Ⓓ

PART 4

Strategy A

Use the questions to focus on a point of view. Listen for words such as
feel or *think*. Point of view is always someone's opinion, not necessarily fact.

> What does the speaker *think* will happen?
> How do the employees *feel* about the changes?
> Did the Board of Directors *agree* with the president?

Test note
In this section of the TOEIC test, be prepared to answer questions
about specific information and details as well as general questions about
the main idea.

Task A

Identify a point of view

**Mark an F next to those sentences that give factual information and an O
next to the sentences that give an opinion.**

1   (A)   The lowest rate that they offer is 9%. ......*F*.....
    (B)   The rate is too high. .....*O*.....
    (C)   You should be able to get a better rate. .....*O*.....

2   (A)   Any complaints should be directed to Mr. Halm. ....
    (B)   Not everyone will be satisfied. ....
    (C)   All requests for changes need to be submitted in writing. ....

3   (A)   Before being promoted, employees must have a review with a manager. ....
    (B)   No one should be promoted before they have completed two years of
          service with the company. ....
    (C)   It seems as though the promotion policy is out of date. ....

4   (A)   The college sent out its catalogue to more than 20,000 interested
          applicants. ....
    (B)   Detailed information about different fields of study is presented in the
          pamphlet. ....
    (C)   The catalogue would be more effective in color. ....

5   (A)   The list of assets should include the property acquired in the takeover. ....
    (B)   The value of the assets comes to just under $20 million. ....
    (C)   Although currently strong, the company should increase its amount of
          liquid assets. ....

6   (A)   The federal government needn't be involved in the setting of rates for
          personal loans. ....
    (B)   His chances of being approved for a loan are low. ....
    (C)   He submitted his application over a month ago. ....

Strategy B

Use the questions and answers to identify a situation. Listen for questions that begin with *what*.

What is happening?
What will they do next?
What just happened?

Task B 🎧

Identify the situation

Read the information below. Listen to extracts from four conversations. Identify where each conversation is taking place (A–D) and what the situation is (E–H).

			Location	**Situation**
7	*B*	*H*	(A) at a business meeting	(E) interviewing for a job
8	....	....	(B) at a bank	(F) disputing a credit card charge
9	....	....	(C) on the telephone	(G) reviewing an annual budget
10	....	....	(D) at an office	(H) applying for a loan

Review 🎧

Directions: Listen and select the best response to each question.

11 How does the speaker view the current rate of corporate borrowing?

(A) As a benefit to productivity
(B) As a bonus for bankers
(C) As a risk to consumers
(D) As a threat to the economy

12 What do the analysts think about the trend?

(A) It's dangerous.
(B) It's expensive.
(C) It's normal.
(D) It's productive.

13 What does the speaker want the audience to do?

(A) Invest in his factory
(B) Borrow more money
(C) Start new companies
(D) Rethink their lending policies

14 What is the meeting about?

(A) Workers are not taking enough vacation.
(B) Everyone is going to Thailand.
(C) People are too relaxed.
(D) Break periods are too long.

15 What does the CEO think about vacations?

(A) They're too trendy.
(B) They're necessary.
(C) They're expensive.
(D) They're inefficient.

16 What could be said about Ms. Woo?

(A) She takes too many vacations.
(B) She never stops working.
(C) She sets a good example.
(D) She is opening an office in Thailand.

Listening
Part 4
11 Ⓐ Ⓑ Ⓒ Ⓓ
12 Ⓐ Ⓑ Ⓒ Ⓓ
13 Ⓐ Ⓑ Ⓒ Ⓓ
14 Ⓐ Ⓑ Ⓒ Ⓓ
15 Ⓐ Ⓑ Ⓒ Ⓓ
16 Ⓐ Ⓑ Ⓒ Ⓓ

Reading PART 5

Strategy A

Read the sentence quickly to see what part of speech is needed to complete it. Then look at the answer choices and identify the parts of speech. Read the sentence again quickly with the answer choice inserted to make sure that it is the correct choice.

We need to reevaluate our .... patterns.

You can see that the blank precedes a noun (*patterns*) and therefore a word to describe this noun is needed. This could be either an adjective or a noun that acts as an adjective.

(A) spending
(B) spend
(C) spent
(D) spender

(A) The participle is used as an adjective and is the correct answer. (B) and (C) are verb forms and therefore not possible. You can identify that (D) is a noun by the *-er* ending.

Grammar Glossary **Parts of Speech** (p115)   **Word Families** (p119)

Task A

Identify the correct word among the same word family

Write in the correct form of the word given in bold. Then use the list of endings to complete the other forms the base word could make.

-ion -er -or -ing -ive -ed -ity -ial -ment -ance -t -d -ier -ist

1   The company's *production* rate is expected to improve. (**produce**)
Other forms of the word: *product* (n) *produced* (pp) *producing* (g) *producer* (n) *productive* (adj) *productivity* (n)

2   Mr. Marokovich doesn't want to .... the estimates, but he will probably have to. (**revise**)
Other forms of the word: .... (n) .... (n) .... (g) .... (pp)

3   Her start-up company is being .... by a development agency that assists women entrepreneurs. (**finance**)
Other forms of the word: .... (n) .... (g) .... (pp) .... (adj)

4   As a young man, he made a wise .... which made him very wealthy. (**invest**)
Other forms of the word: .... (n) .... (g) .... (pp)

5   The city has a database of .... agencies for high-tech companies. (**lend**)
Other forms of the word: .... (n) .... (g) .... (pp)

6   Even though their .... was not up to expectations, investors still have confidence in the company. (**perform**)
Other forms of the word: .... (n) .... (g) .... (pp)

Strategy B

Read the sentences quickly to look for verbs. Identify the tense of the verbs. When there are multiple verbs within the same sentence, confirm that the verb tenses are logical.

Before he orders the materials, he reviews his inventory.
Before he ordered the materials, he reviewed his inventory.

Both of the sentences above are correct. Reading them quickly, you see two verbs: *order* and *review*. In the first sentence, both verbs are in the simple present. In the second sentence, both verbs are in the past tense.

Task B

Identify the correct sequence of tenses

Write the verb tenses in the correct phrase.
Then, put the phrases in the correct order to make a logical sentence.

7   (A) bought   (B) would have
    so that he .....*B*..... a large enough supply
    he .....*A*..... the extra machines

    He bought the extra machines, so that he would have a large enough supply.

8   (A) suggested   (B) believes   (C) will listen
    but no one .... that
    the accountant .... cutting back travel expenses
    management .... to the advice

    ....

9   (A) doesn't want to   (B) forgot
    and now accounting .... reimburse her for the expenses
    she .... to keep her receipts

    ....

10   (A) were   (B) are shocked   (C) failed
    and now .... at the interest rate they have to pay
    the partners .... in such a hurry to secure the loan
    that they .... to read the fine print

    ....

11   (A) had been done   (B) finished
    they .... the year so strongly
    that the budget, which .... in the fall, was unrealistic

    ....

Review

Directions: Select the best answer to complete the sentence.

12 The Stock Market falls when the unemployment rate ....
   (A) will rise
   (B) rises
   (C) risen
   (D) have risen

13 The company plans to issue .... for the first time next quarter.
   (A) divide
   (B) dividends
   (C) divisive
   (D) divider

14 Hix & Co. will announce sales figures from the last quarter which .... expected to be low.
   (A) will
   (B) is
   (C) are
   (D) were

15 It is up to the head of the division to use the .... funds.
   (A) discretionary
   (B) discreet
   (C) discretion
   (D) discreetly

16 His budget always tends to be .... , which protects his department from unexpected costs.
   (A) inflation
   (B) inflationary
   (C) inflate
   (D) inflated

```
Reading
┌─────────────────────────┐
│        Part 5           │
│  12   Ⓐ Ⓑ Ⓒ Ⓓ          │
│  13   Ⓐ Ⓑ Ⓒ Ⓓ          │
│  14   Ⓐ Ⓑ Ⓒ Ⓓ          │
│  15   Ⓐ Ⓑ Ⓒ Ⓓ          │
│  16   Ⓐ Ⓑ Ⓒ Ⓓ          │
└─────────────────────────┘
```

PART 6

Strategy A

One of the blanks deleted in the passage will require you to read beyond the sentence. You may have to look in other parts of the passage to understand the context.

The package was shipped on December 10, over two weeks ago.
It usually only takes five days to arrive here. I don't know why this shipment was ....

(A) overpriced
(B) damaged
(C) delayed
(D) insured

The correct answer is (C). You know the package is delayed because it should have arrived on December 15 and it still had not arrived by December 24. There are no context clues to support the shipment being overpriced, damaged, or insured.

Task A

Identify the context

Complete the sentences with the correct word from the box. Underline the words that provide the context in each sentence.

break	estimate	total	closes	auditors

1   The bank shuts its doors at 5 p.m. so we must get these deposits in before it
....

2   Add the revenue and subtract the expenses to get the ....

3   I've been working non-stop on this project all day without even taking lunch; I need a ....

4   The directors who reviewed the financial statement questioned the ....
about the accounting procedures.

5   Since we cannot predict the future and we are not sure we can meet our projected sales forecasts, the figures in this report are only an ....

Strategy B

Look out for incorrect determiners, which always precede nouns in a sentence. First, check if the noun is singular or plural, and a count or non-count noun. Then, check if the correct determiner is used.

Determiner	Example
Indefinite article	*a, an*
Definite article	*the*
Demonstratives	*this, that, these, those*
Possessives	*my, his, Sharon's, the schools'*
Quantity words	*many, some, each*
Numerals	*one, second*

Grammar glossary **Adjectives: Determiners (p112)**

Task B

Identify determiners

Underline the correct form of the determiner.

6   *My / The* Mexican stock exchange has had a number of dramatic swings *this / the* year.

7   *A / Some* government laid off 20,000 state telecommunications workers when *those / the* system was privatized.

8   Mary set up a meeting with the budget director to try to increase *her / Mary's* departments' allocation.

9   The financial services company announced that it would open *that / three* new offices this year.

10 *Some / An* Internet company sold *this / its* shares for 150 yen.

Review

Directions: Select the best answer to complete the text.

Questions 11–14 refer to the following brochure.

Park, Lee and Associates started as _____ two-person firm more than 75 years

11   (A) a
       (B) one
       (C) this
       (D) the

ago and has grown into South Korea's largest independent Certified Public Accounting firm. _____ got that way by focusing on the special needs of

12   (A) They
       (B) She
       (C) We
       (D) It

our clients. We always put the client first. We offer traditional accounting services such as audit and tax services. We also act as consultants and can provide a number of new, innovative services such as fund start-up services. We help business owners save money and protect themselves from risk. We help individuals protect _____ assets, plan for the future, and minimize taxes.

13   (A) our
       (B) her
       (C) its
       (D) their

_____ services set us apart from other firms.

14   (A) This
       (B) That
       (C) These
       (D) The

With clients throughout South Korea and in more than two dozen countries, Park, Lee and Associates combines the resources of a large public accounting firm with the personal attention of a small organization.

Reading

Part 6

11	Ⓐ	Ⓑ	Ⓒ	Ⓓ
12	Ⓐ	Ⓑ	Ⓒ	Ⓓ
13	Ⓐ	Ⓑ	Ⓒ	Ⓓ
14	Ⓐ	Ⓑ	Ⓒ	Ⓓ

PART 7

Strategy A

Use the question and answer choices to focus on the sequence of events.
Read the question and answer choices quickly before reading the passage.
Look for time-sequence markers to indicate in what order events take place.

Time-sequence markers
Look for the following types of words to indicate the order of events.
*before   after   at the same time   following   first
then   in order to   prior to   finally   until*

What should the recipient do first?
(A)   Cancel his/her credit card   (C)   Contact the company
(B)   Wait 90 days to use the card   (D)   Make the payment

We regret to inform you that we will be forced to cancel your credit card if we do not receive payment within the next 15 days. The balance on your account has been outstanding for over 90 days. While we value you as an important customer, we cannot overlook this. Until we receive payment, you will be unable to use your card. Upon payment, you will once again be able to enjoy all the benefits of being a cardholder.

(D) is the correct answer. The word *first* in the question indicates that you need to identify a sequence of events. (A) This is something that the *sender* will do, not the *recipient*. (B) This refers to a past event – the 90-day lateness of payment. It is not something that anyone *should do*. (C) Contacting the company sounds logical, but it is not mentioned in the notice. (D) The recipient should make payment within the next 15 days. Therefore (D) is the correct answer.

Task A

Identify the sequence of events

Read a sentence from a passage and choose the best answer.

1   Following the intense and prolonged negotiations, she took a three-week vacation.
    What happened first?

    (A) She went on vacation.
    (B) She finished the negotiations.
    (C) She prolonged the negotiations.

2   In order to make accurate predictions, they must first have the historical data and the competitor's information.
    When is it possible to make good predictions?

    (A) When they have both types of data
    (B) After they get the historical data
    (C) Before they have the competitor's information

3   If the company doesn't invest in a new computer system soon, it won't be able to produce accurate reports with the tremendous amount of information it is receiving.
    What should the company do immediately?

    (A) Purchase a new system
    (B) Get more information
    (C) Publish the reports

4   Before we begin making any final changes, everyone should go back and check the figures that have been submitted.
    What should be done now?

    (A) Everyone should change their numbers.
    (B) They should verify the numbers.
    (C) The final product should be determined.

Strategy B

Look for questions that include words such as *must*, *need to*, and *necessary* to identify questions that ask for requirements. Often requirements are listed together. Questions about requirements are very specific, so you can read the passage quickly to locate exactly the information that is asked for.

What *must* employees do before the training session?
What does the group *need to* submit to the bank official?
What items are *necessary* for a successful opening?

What must the reader do if she is interested?
(A)   Have access to a computer
(B)   Wait a short period of time
(C)   Establish good credit
(D)   Give the names of some people she knows

Technological changes have made it easier for individuals to take charge of their personal finances. Now you can access all of the information you need, in just minutes!
Join **FinaForm Infoquest** and secure your future now.

At **FinaForm Infoquest** you can access the lowest finance rates for houses, automobiles, even college education! You can enter the stock market, assisted by our expert traders. You can invest in bonds and mutual funds. All of this access is available to you at a very low cost, and it is easier than you think. All you need to do is to provide us with a statement of annual income, two credit references, and a list of four friends or acquaintances who might be interested in our services. Don't delay, call today!

(D) is the correct answer. The question asks for requirements. You should read the passage quickly and look for the section where the requirements are listed. You see the word *need* and a list at the end of the passage, so you will likely find requirements listed here. (A) This is never mentioned in the passage, although you might connect technological changes with computers. (B) *Time* is referred to at the beginning of the passage, but *waiting* is not one of the requirements. (C) *Credit* is mentioned at the end of the passage, where the requirements are listed. However, the passage doesn't say what kind of credit history is needed. (D) The *names of people* refers to *friends and acquaintances*, so this option is the correct answer.

Task B

Identify requirements

Cross out the words that are NOT a requirement for the item underlined.

5   loan application
    bank statement, résumé, identification, education, annual income, credit references

6   credit card
    phone number, height, tax bracket, billing address, credit history, debt

7   annual report
    overall performance, projections, Board of Directors, gross sales, paychecks, invoice

8   weekly meeting
    agenda, attendance, minutes, hiring manual, leader, waiting period

9   budgets
    low prices, allocation of funds, employee salaries, interest rates, housing loan, estimates

10 balance sheet
    assets, letter of recommendation, company background, debits, liabilities, legal assistance

Strategy C

In the double passage set, you may have to identify the reason something happened. The cause may be in the first passage and the effect in the second passage. These questions often begin with *why*.

Why did the stock price fall?

    (A) A merger was announced.
    (B) The company declared bankruptcy.
    (C) The CEO was put in jail.
    (D) Earnings were less than projected.

Quarterly Report

	Projected	Actual
Cash	$0.24m	$0.24m
Expenses	$12.6m	$13.5m
Revenue	$38.5m	$15.6m

Mano Ltd. announced today that it was taking measures to stop the recent slide in its stock price. Financial analysts discount the rumors that this change in stock price is due to the fact that the company is close to bankruptcy and that CEO Gordon Jones is under investigation for tax evasion. Rumors that the company will merge with TyLo are unfounded. We believe that the cause can be easily found in this quarter's financial statement released yesterday.

(D) is the correct answer. The news article suggests that the reason for the decrease in stock prices can be found in the quarterly report, which shows that the actual revenues are less than half what was projected. (A), (B), and (C) These options were mentioned in the news article as false rumors.

Task C

Identify a reason

Match the reasons (11–15) with the statements (A–E).

11   The company was overstaffed.

12   The president wanted to reward the departments that performed well.

13   The price of luxury goods has not increased.

14   Interest rates on credit cards have gone from 18% to 10%.

15   A computer thief stole some of our financial data.

(A)   People are purchasing less with cash and charging more.

(B)   The advertising manager and her team were given an extra week's vacation.

(C)   We changed our accounting system to one which offers more protection.

(D)   In spite of fuel increases, the cost of a private jet was stable this year.

(E)   A few employees were made redundant.

Review

Directions: Read the memo and the email and select the best answer for each question.

Questions 16–20 refer to the following memo and email.

> *To:*   Department Heads
> *From:*   Charlene Boyer, CEO
> *Date:*   August 1
> *Subject:*   Budget Review Committee
>
> It's that time of year again! Many of you have already begun work on your department's budget for next year. In an attempt to make the process smoother and more satisfactory for everyone involved, we are making some changes to the process.
>
> As usual, department heads are asked to submit preliminary budgets to the Executive Committee by August 15. This year, we want to involve more employees in the process. A special committee will review the budgets. This committee will consist of four members of the Executive Committee and two representatives from each department.
>
> As department heads, you will choose your own representatives to the committee. They must be able to contribute 10 hours a week for a month. Please submit their names by August 7. No names submitted after that date will be considered.

To:	Charlene Boyer, CEO
From:	Lawrence Redding, Sales and Marketing Director
Date:	August 12
Subject:	Re: Budget Review Committee

I would like to propose my leading sales representative, JoEllen Corcoran, to be a member of the Budget Review Committee. Although she has a full work schedule, I will adjust her schedule so she can be free 10 hours a week for a month. She'll be going on vacation in two months, but I imagine the process will be finished before she leaves. She helped our department determine the budget so she is well qualified to review budgets submitted by other departments.

16 What is required of the representatives?

    (A) They must be a member of the Executive Committee.
    (B) They must submit a budget by August 15.
    (C) They must be the department head.
    (D) They must be willing to spend 40 hours on this project in one month.

17 How does Ms. Boyer feel about the budget process?

    (A) Only the top management should be involved.
    (B) It can't be improved.
    (C) It should be a more open process.
    (D) It's time to finalize the budget.

18 Who decided on the budgets last year?

    (A) Departments, through democratic vote
    (B) Representatives from each department
    (C) The Executive Committee
    (D) The department heads

19 What will happen next?

    (A) A list of names will be given to Ms. Boyer.
    (B) The initial budgets will be turned in.
    (C) The Executive Committee will meet.
    (D) The process will be smoother.

20 Why will Ms. Corcoran probably not be a member of the Budget Review Committee?

    (A) She's going on vacation.
    (B) Her name was submitted late.
    (C) She's never worked on a budget before.
    (D) She's too busy.

Reading

Part 7				
16	Ⓐ	Ⓑ	Ⓒ	Ⓓ
17	Ⓐ	Ⓑ	Ⓒ	Ⓓ
18	Ⓐ	Ⓑ	Ⓒ	Ⓓ
19	Ⓐ	Ⓑ	Ⓒ	Ⓓ
20	Ⓐ	Ⓑ	Ⓒ	Ⓓ

Chapter 3 Housing and Property

Listening PART 1

Strategy A

Use the pictures to identify physical relationships. Look at the pictures carefully and ask yourself *where* an object is in relation to another object or person.

Where?
The contractor is holding a pipe in his right hand.
The contractor is holding the plans in his left hand.

Where?
The sign is next to the sidewalk.
The sign is at the edge of the lawn.

Grammar Glossary **Prepositions of Location** (p116)

Task A

Identify the physical relationship between objects

Underline the correct preposition to describe the most probable relationship between the objects.

1   The doorknob is *on / in* the right side of the glass door.

2   The housekeeper pointed to the broken window *above / on top of* the sofa.

3   The apartment was located *near / within* a bus stop.

4   The building manager took out the keys which were hidden *under / in front of* the desk in a small drawer.

5   The crane is sitting directly *in front of / around* our offices.

Strategy B

Be aware of answer choices that are irrelevant. The TOEIC® test often uses answer choices that are not relevant to the photo. Make a quick mental list of what you see in the pictures. In the first picture below this might include: *blueprints*, *papers*, *drawings*, *people*, *architects*, *engineers*. Look for related vocabulary in the answer choices. Ask yourself what parts of the wrong answers are relevant and what parts are irrelevant.

(A) She's cutting lumber for a house.	(A) The painter is sanding the walls.
(B) The building is underground.	(B) The plumber is fixing the leak.
(C) She's discussing the plans.	(C) The electrician is wiring the ceiling.
(D) They're buying new hard hats.	(D) The carpenter is on the roof.

The correct answer is (C).   The correct answer is (D).

Task B

Identify irrelevancies

Cross out the word that is NOT related to all of the other words. Tell why.

6   screw, hammer, screwdriver, hardware store, nail

   ....

7   wall, ceiling, carpet, door, window

   ....

8   ladder, wheelbarrow, scaffold, crane, stairs

   ....

9   constructing, building, erecting, demolishing, putting up

   ....

10   owning, renting, leasing, hiring, letting

   ....

Review 🎧

Directions: Listen and select the one statement that best describes what you see in the picture.

11

12

13

14

Listening
Part 1
11 Ⓐ Ⓑ Ⓒ Ⓓ
12 Ⓐ Ⓑ Ⓒ Ⓓ
13 Ⓐ Ⓑ Ⓒ Ⓓ
14 Ⓐ Ⓑ Ⓒ Ⓓ

PART 2

Strategy A

Listen for questions that ask *what* to identify things.

What is the man looking at?
What is the problem with the building?
What does the woman have in her hands?
What delayed the construction?

Task A

Identify things

Cross out the answer choices that are NOT possible.

1   What is the man carrying?

    (A)   I believe it is the ladder.
    (B)   It is a tape measure.
    (C)   He has a hard-hat on his head.

2   What is behind the office?

    (A)   An adjoining office.
    (B)   There is nothing there yet.
    (C)   The store is in front.

3   What is being stored next to the supplies?

    (A)   They belong to the previous owner.
    (B)   Just an old computer.
    (C)   There is nothing there right now.

4   What is the going rate for new property in this area?

    (A)   The prices vary greatly.
    (B)   It's approximately $3.50 per square foot.
    (C)   The vacancy level is very high.

5   What equipment does she need for her work?

    (A)   She made a lot of money last year.
    (B)   It varies from project to project.
    (C)   A drafting table and some good pencils.

6   What is the problem with the new lights?

    (A)   The switch doesn't work properly.
    (B)   They were installed over a month ago.
    (C)   The wires were crossed by accident.

7   What is next on her agenda?

    (A)   A brief meeting and then lunch.
    (B)   She is planning to visit the site.
    (C)   The agents were pleased with the visits.

8   What are the superintendent's main responsibilities?

    (A)   He doesn't earn enough.
    (B)   Taking care of all of the units and overseeing the staff.
    (C)   Maintenance, repairs and general assistance.

9   What is causing the delay?

    (A)   The materials haven't arrived.
    (B)   They will commence work at 1:00.
    (C)   There is a bad accident on the highway.

10   What is the main problem with the old facility?

    (A)   They say that it is valued at over $5 million.
    (B)   The plumbing can't be used any longer.
    (C)   It has extensive water damage from the flood last year.

Strategy B

Listen for questions that ask for the status of a situation.
The status indicates whether something is finished, being worked on, postponed, forgotten, etc.

Is the project *finished*?
When will they sign the lease?
Why *is she making another* trip to the new facilities?

Task B

Identify the status of the situation

Mark the sentences that indicate a situation that is finished with a *F*, a situation that is being worked on with a *WO* and others with an *O*.

11 (A) The president reconsidered the project when he saw the initial plans. ....*O*....
    (B) That was wrapped up last week. ....*F*.....
    (C) They want to finalize everything before the construction begins. ....*WO*...

12 (A) All of the art was hung last night. ....
    (B) There are five remaining pieces to arrange. ....
    (C) Unfortunately, that project was pushed to the back of the line. ....

13 (A) They've been working all day on a final decision. ....
    (B) In a vote of five to four, the project was approved. ....
    (C) Although the deadline is tomorrow, they only started discussions yesterday. ....

14 (A) The bank has been analyzing the company's credit history for the building loan. ....
    (B) The bank went out of business while they were in the process of reviewing the application. ....
    (C) The records say that that file was closed months ago. ....

15 (A) By granting the final seal of approval, they were finally able to put the building behind them. ....
    (B) We've sent the plans to the contractor's office and they're dealing with them. ....
    (C) They were unable to come to a consensus. ....

Review 🎧

Directions: Listen and select the best response to the question or statement.

Listening			
Part 2			
16	Ⓐ	Ⓑ	Ⓒ
17	Ⓐ	Ⓑ	Ⓒ
18	Ⓐ	Ⓑ	Ⓒ
19	Ⓐ	Ⓑ	Ⓒ
20	Ⓐ	Ⓑ	Ⓒ
21	Ⓐ	Ⓑ	Ⓒ
22	Ⓐ	Ⓑ	Ⓒ
23	Ⓐ	Ⓑ	Ⓒ
24	Ⓐ	Ⓑ	Ⓒ
25	Ⓐ	Ⓑ	Ⓒ

PART 3

Strategy A

Use the questions and answers to identify a recommendation or a suggestion.
Look for words such as *recommend*, *suggest* or *should* and *could*.

> What does the man *recommend* that the woman do?
> How *should* the man react?
> What *could* the speakers do?
> How does Susan *suggest* that they leave?

Task A 🎧

Identify a recommendation or suggestion

Listen to five conversations and check the choice that best finishes each conversation with an appropriate suggestion or recommendation.

1. (A) Why don't you send him a memo about it?
    (B) It shouldn't take more than four months.
    (C) I would start looking again.
    (D) He has had problems before with his vision.

2. (A) You should verify the type of payment.
    (B) We bought fifteen just last week.
    (C) You might think about renting.
    (D) Why don't you find a music group?

3. (A) Area commercial property should increase in price.
    (B) The downtown area is undergoing a renovation.
    (C) Let's redecorate.
    (D) It's time to start looking for new space.

4. (A) I have to leave in a couple of minutes.
    (B) Rob is the new owner.
    (C) You should try to attend. It's important.
    (D) You can tell me about it tomorrow.

5. (A) The last group bought a lot of merchandise.
    (B) I would invite them back next week.
    (C) We should increase the asking price.
    (D) It would be better to show them one at a time.

Strategy B

Look for questions that ask to identify a request. Look for questions that begin with *what*. Make sure you choose the request for the correct speaker.

What does the woman want the man to do?
What will the speaker request?
What did the customer ask for?

Task B 🎧

Identify requests

Listen to extracts from four conversations. Then underline the answer choice that correctly identifies the request.

6   What is the labor union asking for?
    (A) It is always changing.
    (B) They want better medical benefits and higher salaries.
    (C) The man doesn't know.
    (D) It is asking for more help.

7   What is the speaker requesting?
    (A) Material to mail to clients
    (B) The right to hang up notices
    (C) Larger offices
    (D) Lower mail rates

8   What is being requested?
    (A) A lowering of the rent
    (B) An extension of the lease
    (C) A deduction in the yearly payments
    (D) More space

9   What is the city requesting?
    (A) A measurement of the site
    (B) Early completion of the project
    (C) Removal of all the debris
    (D) A listing of all materials

Review 🎧

Directions: Listen and select the best response to each question.

10 When did they expect the permit to be issued?
    (A) June 1
    (B) June 5
    (C) Around June 19
    (D) July 10

11 What does the man want the woman to do?
    (A) See if the mayor's office can get the permit issued
    (B) Start construction on the project
    (C) Approve the application
    (D) Wait another six weeks

12 What does the woman suggest they do next?
    (A) Start construction without the permits
    (B) Contact the permit office
    (C) Make trouble for the mayor
    (D) Submit the permit application again

13 What does the woman think the man could do?
    (A) Spend more time commuting
    (B) Try working from home
    (C) Talk on the phone less
    (D) Answer his emails

14 What does the woman want the man to do?
    (A) Return phone calls
    (B) Work less on the computer
    (C) Stop telecommuting
    (D) Request permission to work at home

15 What does the woman think about meetings?
    (A) They bring people together.
    (B) They waste time.
    (C) They encourage group participation.
    (D) They can be done from home.

Listening			
Part 3			
10	Ⓐ Ⓑ Ⓒ Ⓓ		
11	Ⓐ Ⓑ Ⓒ Ⓓ		
12	Ⓐ Ⓑ Ⓒ Ⓓ		
13	Ⓐ Ⓑ Ⓒ Ⓓ		
14	Ⓐ Ⓑ Ⓒ Ⓓ		
15	Ⓐ Ⓑ Ⓒ Ⓓ		

PART 4

Strategy A

Use the questions and answers to focus on a problem and the reason for the problem. Look for questions that begin with *why* and *what*. Read the questions and answer choices quickly to identify the information that you need.

> *Why* are they having a meeting?
> *What* is the purpose of the meeting?
> *What* is the problem?

Notice that these questions don't ask for details. They are asking for the main idea.

Task A 🎧

Identify the problem

You will hear three talks. Before each talk begins, read the answer choices quickly. Then listen and cross out the answer choices that are NOT possible.

1   Why are they meeting?

    (A) To solve a problem
    (B) To create a plan of action
    (C) To complain to the city council
    (D) To reduce the number of criminals

2   What is the problem?

    (A) There are fewer cinemas.
    (B) Robberies and homicides have increased.
    (C) There are too many buyers.
    (D) Frightened people don't buy property.

3   What is the purpose of the advertisement?

    (A) To raise interest in commercial space
    (B) To announce full occupancy
    (C) To entice buyers
    (D) To promote an office complex

4   What is the problem?

    (A) Space is limited.
    (B) No more appointments are available.
    (C) Offices are only for rent.
    (D) Time is short.

5   Why have the people gathered?

    (A) They want to go swimming.
    (B) They rented an apartment on the third floor.
    (C) They want to tour an apartment complex.
    (D) They are interested in a place to live.

6   What is a drawback to the complex?

    (A) There are only three floors.
    (B) It is under construction.
    (C) There are no recreational facilities.
    (D) The swimming pool isn't ready yet.

Strategy B

Use the questions and answers to identify solutions to problems. Solutions generally come after the problem has been identified.

Due to low attendance, we will reschedule the meeting for next month. Details will be sent to you in the mail. We apologize for any inconvenience.

The problem isn't stated directly, but you can guess that the problem is that they had to cancel a meeting. The problem is referred to *due to low attendance* and is followed by a solution *we will reschedule*.

Task B 🎧

Identify possible solutions

Listen to four talks and identify possible solutions. Cross out the answer choices that do NOT present possible solutions.

7
(A)   The police department will not listen to a group of realtors.
(B)   The realtors can submit individual plans.
(C)   The realtors invite criminals to help them.
(D)   The plan demands more police on the street.

8
(A)   There'll always be another chance.
(B)   More than one hundred offices can still be built.
(C)   30% of the space is still available.
(D)   Appointments can still be made.

9
(A)   People can go to a nearby gym to use a pool.
(B)   They can park at a local facility.
(C)   Tenants may rent a three-bedroom apartment.
(D)   Most tenants don't want to swim now anyway.

10
(A)   Roads will not be repaired.
(B)   Property tax will be increased.
(C)   A committee will study the problem.
(D)   The Council will close the schools.

Test Note
Once you identify a problem, you should anticipate possible solutions. Don't, however, choose an answer that is not mentioned in the talk. In order for the answer to be correct, it must be stated or inferred in the listening.

Review 🎧

Directions: Listen and select the best response to each question.

11   What is the purpose of this announcement?
(A)   To announce a change in ownership
(B)   To discuss property values
(C)   To make customer referrals
(D)   To introduce a service

12   What problem do the managers have?
(A)   They don't know how to manage.
(B)   They don't have enough time.
(C)   They aren't making any money.
(D)   They can't keep employees busy.

13   How can the speaker help?
(A)   By giving low-cost loans
(B)   By finding good properties
(C)   By providing property managers
(D)   By referring other business

---

14   Why is the speaker making the announcement?
(A)   To present a plan of action
(B)   To announce a retirement package
(C)   To congratulate a good painter
(D)   To improve morale

15   What specifically is the problem?
(A)   Only 40% occupancy rate
(B)   No vacancies
(C)   Wet paint
(D)   Unclean apartments

16   What does the speaker suggest everyone do?
(A)   Work independently
(B)   Go to the marina
(C)   Take no vacation for the next 14 days
(D)   Take some time off

Listening				
Part 4				
11	Ⓐ	Ⓑ	ⓒ	Ⓓ
12	Ⓐ	Ⓑ	ⓒ	Ⓓ
13	Ⓐ	Ⓑ	ⓒ	Ⓓ
14	Ⓐ	Ⓑ	ⓒ	Ⓓ
15	Ⓐ	Ⓑ	ⓒ	Ⓓ
16	Ⓐ	Ⓑ	ⓒ	Ⓓ

Reading PART 5

Grammar Glossary **Cause and Effect** (p113)

Task A

Identify cause and effect

Mark *C* over the phrase or clause that is the cause, and *E* over the phrase or clause that is the effect.

1   The group of realtors wasn't able to sell the buildings, because of the structural faults that were discovered.

2   During the emergency training, the building complex is evacuated after the water main breaks and the bundle of loose wires catches on fire.

3   The quality of our properties improves constantly because of the intense level of competition in the surrounding areas.

4   Because of a shortage of office space, rents were very high.

5   Snow was not cleared from the parking lot, because the snow plough was being repaired.

6   Due to the unusually cold weather, the management turned on the heat.

Strategy B

Identify the verbs in the sentence and mark *S* if they are stative or *NS* if they are non-stative. Stative verbs usually do not take the progressive (*-ing*) form.

It .... from their discussions as though the earliest date for the contract to be signed is November 25.
(A)   is sounding
(B)   sounding
(C)   sound
(D)   sounds

The correct answer is (D). You can quickly see from the answer choices that the verb to be used is *sound*. *Sound* is a stative verb and therefore does not take the progressive form. Therefore you can quickly eliminate answer choices (A) and (B). You see that with *it*, you need the third person singular *-s*, so that answer choice (C) can also be eliminated.

Grammar Glossary   **Verbs: Stative**   (p117)

Task B

Identify stative verbs

Check the grammatically correct sentence. Mark S by the stative verbs or NS by the non-stative verbs.

       S

7   (A)   It *seems* that the executive committee liked the plans for the expansion. ✓

   (B)   It *is seeming* that the executive committee likes the plans for the expansion.

8   (A)   Developers *are appearing* more and more frequently at the city council meetings.

   (B)   Developers *appear* more and more frequently at the city council meetings.

9   (A)   Even though he is exhausted, he *is working* all night to finish the project.

   (B)   Even though he is exhausted, he *works* all night to finish the project.

10   (A)   Even though the deal fell through, the project manager *was sensing* that another deal was possible.

   (B)   Even though the deal fell through, the project manager *sensed* that another deal was possible.

11   (A)   We *are wanting* to give you a tour of the property if you are interested.

   (B)   We *want* to give you a tour of the property if you are interested.

Review

Directions: Select the best answer to complete the sentence.

12 Her finishing our design plans .... on her other projects.

    (A) is depending
    (B) depend
    (C) depends
    (D) is depended

13 The owners, by signing the agreement, ... to the neighborhood renovation project.

    (A) is committing
    (B) commits
    (C) commit
    (D) are committing

14 The new manager .... to the east coast.

    (A) are transfer
    (B) is transferring
    (C) transfers
    (D) are transferring

15 Fifteen hundred pounds of cement .... to arrive tomorrow for the housing project.

    (A) are
    (B) am
    (C) being
    (D) is

16 The lawyer, but not the client, ... that the lease is fair.

    (A) is feeling
    (B) feels
    (C) feel
    (D) are feeling

Reading

Part 5				
12	Ⓐ	Ⓑ	Ⓒ	Ⓓ
13	Ⓐ	Ⓑ	Ⓒ	Ⓓ
14	Ⓐ	Ⓑ	Ⓒ	Ⓓ
15	Ⓐ	Ⓑ	Ⓒ	Ⓓ
16	Ⓐ	Ⓑ	Ⓒ	Ⓓ

PART 6

Strategy A

In the TOEIC test, you may see answer choices which contain a gerund or an infinitive. Ask yourself which is required. Some verbs are followed by a gerund, while others are followed by an infinitive. Yet others may be followed by either.

She couldn't imagine .... far from her job.
- (A) to live
- (B) living
- (C) live
- (D) lived

(B) is the correct answer. The verb *imagine* is followed by a gerund.

Remember: some verbs can be followed by either a gerund or an infinitive.

He *remembered asking* the building manager about the availability.
He *remembered to ask* the building manager about the availability.

In the examples above, both sentences are correct. However, they have different meanings, depending on the form.

> **Grammar Glossary** Gerunds and Infinitives (p114)

Task A

Identify the appropriate use of the gerund or the infinitive

Underline the correct form of the verb.

1   The bank advised the property owners *giving / to give* an accurate appraisal of the property.

2   The landlord expected *to receive / receiving* the rent checks on the first of the month.

3   The rental agent hopes *to convince / convincing* the client that other renters want the property.

4   They are considering *bringing in / to bring in* additional staff to manage the property during the peak summer months.

5   The chairman wanted *stopping / to stop* cost overruns.

Strategy B

Use the commas and conjunctions in the passage to help you complete the sentence. If you find a series of phrases in the sentence, such as a group of nouns, prepositional phrases, or verbs, you will need the same part of speech to complete the sentence.

The firm was unable to draw the plans or .... the building within their budget.
- (A) construction
- (B) construct
- (C) constructing
- (D) constructor

(B) is the correct answer. The conjunction *and* connects two verbs and these phrases form a parallel structure. Both verbs need to be in the base form.

Grammar Glossary Parallel Structures (p115)

Task B

Identify the parallel structures

Mark *C* over the conjunction and write the type of phrases used (noun, adjective or prepositional phrase). Then underline the phrase that does not follow the parallel structure.

6   The zoning regulations state that restaurants, <u>office build</u>, and any other
     commercial properties are strictly prohibited in the area. *noun phrases*

7   Some of the special features include exercise facilitation on the premises, dry-
     cleaning services, and a convenience store. ....

8   Stage three required finishing touches the walls, on the restrooms, and above
     the entrances and exits. ....

9   We suggested that they place the "For Rent" signs on the windows, front lawn
     or at the coffee shop. ....

10   The combination of the new airport, increased traffic, and rising crime rated
     have resulted in lower property values. ....

11   The rates included water and gas but not electrify. ....

12   I can only show the property in the evening or the weekend. ....

13   The realtor described the apartment as open, bright and sun. ....

14   Our corporate exercise program includes strength building, aerobic training,
     and weights. ....

15   The downtown properties tend to be small, dark and depression in comparison
     to the bright and open suburban properties. ....

Review

Directions: Select the best answer to complete the text.

Questions 16–19 refer to the following newspaper article.

Shipping containers become homes

Many countries need emergency shelter for people left homeless after floods, earthquakes, and other natural disasters. Discarded shipping containers, which fit on the back of a flat-bed truck, usually see service from the road to the dock and then across the seas. Now, in many parts of the world, they are being recycled and used as _____ homes. They fill a short-term need for victims of natural

16 (A) temporary
(B) short
(C) vacation
(D) second

disasters until more permanent homes can be built.

In some countries, these containers are becoming permanent homes. For example, in Western Europe, they are being turned into fashionable, contemporary _____. Some container homes can have two or more stories, terraces, patios,

17 (A) resident
(B) residences
(C) residential
(D) residing

and even indoor swimming pools.

Containers not only serve as homes for people in need of emergency shelter, they are also being used _____ mobile museums. One Japanese architect designed

18 (A) to
(B) for
(C) since
(D) as

an enormous museum made of containers to exhibit a photographer's work. Both the photography exhibition and the container-museum traveled around the world.

You can read more about container homes by typing in Pre-Fab homes on a web search engine and _____ on any reference to container dwellings.

19 (A) click
(B) to click
(C) clicking
(D) is clicking

Reading

Part 6

16 Ⓐ Ⓑ Ⓒ Ⓓ
17 Ⓐ Ⓑ Ⓒ Ⓓ
18 Ⓐ Ⓑ Ⓒ Ⓓ
19 Ⓐ Ⓑ Ⓒ Ⓓ

PART 7

Realtors Plus is a monthly publication aimed at serving the needs of the local realtor community. Our job requires us to work intensely with our customers and leaves us little time to work with our colleagues. Many of us view our colleagues not as colleagues, but as competition. Our aim is to change that attitude and create a true community, whereby all of us can benefit and grow our businesses. We accomplish this aim by focusing on market research, inside tips, and providing a "Best Practices" feature section.

Realtors Plus will begin publication in July. It will also be available on line the fifth of every month. You may subscribe at www.realtorsplus.com for a low monthly fee of $6.50. Come join our community!

The correct answer is (C). In order to answer this question correctly, you need to understand the overall aim of the notice. While realtors often work with first-time homebuyers, the advertisement does not mention or address these buyers, so (A) does not answer the question. (B) refers vaguely to *aggressive competitors*. This notice specifically refers to the opportunity for building relationships as colleagues, not as competitors, so (B) is incorrect. (D) repeats the word *community* from the notice, but this is not the targeted reader of the advertisement. The ad is a sales notice for a new publication serving the needs of the *local realtor community*.

Task A

Identify the target audience

Choose the answer choice that identifies the most probable target audience.

1   You're reading a notice about an eviction. Who is the likely target audience?
    (A) The burglars
    (B) The apartment manager
    (C) The tenants
    (D) A national politician

2   You're reading a report on dropping occupancy rates in the city. Who is the likely target audience?
    (A) Prospective buyers
    (B) Farmers
    (C) Factory owners
    (D) Busy groups

3   You're reading a letter outlining problems in the building such as garbage removal, water leaks, and excessive noise. Who is the likely target audience?
    (A) Home owners
    (B) A building superintendent
    (C) The city council
    (D) An environmental group

4   You are reading an advertisement for an apartment building security device? Who is the likely target audience?
    (A) The military
    (B) A corporate operations manager
    (C) An apartment renter
    (D) A security company

Strategy B

Read the answer choices and passage quickly to look for adjectives and details to identify an event or an activity.

What event is being announced?
(A)   A discussion about scheduling   (C)   An international bazaar
(B)   Interviews to find new managers   (D)   A meeting of managers

> Mark your calendars now if you haven't already for the semi-annual gathering of our top managers from around the world. For those of you who have attended the meeting in the past, you know the preparation that we put into the meeting and the value and information that you take away from it. For those of you for whom this will be the first meeting, welcome and congratulations!
>
> We are very careful in our selection process. Each manager must be nominated from a group of peers and supervisors. In addition, each manager has at least a 20% growth record for the past three years. Your inclusion to this year's meeting is to be congratulated.

(D) is the correct answer. Looking at the question and the answer choices, you see that you are trying to identify an event. (A) plays on the first sentence in the notice, *Mark your calendars*. However, readers are asked to mark their calendars in order to remember the meeting, not because the meeting is for scheduling purposes. (B) mentions managers, as does the passage, but there is no mention of hiring new managers. (C) uses the word *international*, which is similar in meaning to *around the world* in the passage. However, the notice is not about a bazaar. The passage is announcing a gathering, or meeting, of managers, so (D) is the correct answer.

Task B

Identify the activity or event

Cross out the answer choices that do NOT describe what might be included in the event or activity.

5   Open House
(A)   The public is invited.
(B)   Apartments are available to view.
(C)   The families in 2D and 5C changed apartments.
(D)   The restaurant closed its doors.

6   A seminar on finding the best vendors for property managers
(A)   A list of companies in the area
(B)   Good and bad examples
(C)   Services an electrician should provide
(D)   The hours for the exercise facilities

7   Auction of public lands
(A)   Held on Saturday, April 25, at 10:00 a.m.
(B)   Free for the first ten customers
(C)   Great prices
(D)   Photos of antiques

8   New tax laws
(A)   Costly political campaign
(B)   Commercial property in residential area
(C)   Intense public debate
(D)   Increased airport taxes

9   A training session for the housekeeping staff
(A)   Owners discuss new properties.
(B)   Everyone must read the safety manual.
(C)   A new childcare center opened on Main Street.
(D)   New cleaning materials have been purchased.

10   A workshop on housing changes
(A)   Construction of single family units has been stopped.
(B)   The subway system has lessened traffic.
(C)   The city is undergoing a revitalization.
(D)   New homeowners can qualify for loans.

Strategy C

One of the questions in the double passage set may ask you to identify a difference in time. Read the questions and answer choices quickly. Look for questions about time and decide if you will need information from both passages to answer the question. These questions usually begin with *when*.

1. When will the city commission receive the first concept design?
   (A) February
   (B) March
   (C) April
   (D) May

Proposed schedule

January 10	Committee prepares specifications for architect
January 20	Committee meets with architect to review specifications
February 10	Architect delivers first design to committee
February 20	Architect submits revised design to city for approval
March 15	City commission reviews first concept design
May 30	City commission provides feedback to architect
June 10	Architect submits plans to city building department

Building Committee Minutes, March 15

The chairperson of the building committee reported today that we were behind in our schedule. The revisions were more detailed than anticipated. Consequently, the city will not receive the first concept drawings as planned. Delivery will be postponed to the commission's meeting next month.

(C) is the correct answer. The city commission was to have received the first design on March 15, but this has been postponed for one month (until April) while the design is revised. (A), (B), and (D) February, March, and May are all mentioned in the schedule but are not the correct answer.

Task C

Identify a time

Match the statements (11–15) with the times (A–E).

11 1 The lease on our office space expires in six months.
    2 The landlord gave us a six-month extension on our lease.

12 1 When the weather is cold, people want to keep warm.
    2 Our sales of heaters increase in January through March.

13 1 We had 25 chairs in the conference room this morning.
    2 We're expecting 35 people at noon.

14 1 We've been in the same location for ten years.
    2 Before we moved here, we worked out of our home for two years.

15 1 The realtor can't show the building until tomorrow.
    2 The potential buyer is leaving town today and won't return until next week.

(A) We've been in business for 12 years.

(B) We can stay where we are for one more year.

(C) We need ten more chairs before 12 p.m.

(D) Sales in the first quarter are strong.

(E) They won't see the property for at least seven days.

Review

Directions: Read the announcement and the flyer and select the best answer for each question.

Questions 16–20 refer to the following announcement and flyer.

There will be a town meeting at the Wetlands Community Center on Manchester Blvd. on Saturday at 9:00 a.m. We encourage all citizens to get involved in the community and to attend the meeting. Speakers from the development company and an environmental group will be discussing the pros and cons of the proposed industrial and residential areas.

The City Manager's Office will be taking up the issue of development in sessions beginning next month. Before that happens, we feel that the community needs to be well informed so that we can, in turn, guide our leaders in the action that they take. The future of our community very much depends on the outcome of this current debate.

Breakfast will be served. We ask everyone to bring a list of questions and concerns to be presented to the speakers. We look forward to seeing you there. Remember, our community's future is in your hands!

We will distribute the agenda for the meeting by the end of the week. That flyer will confirm the details of the meeting.

What?	Town meeting
Who?	All citizens of Wetlands
Where?	Oakland Elementary School, Dixie Highway
When?	Saturday, April 12, 9:00–11:30 a.m.

AGENDA

9:00 a.m.	Breakfast Meet and greet your neighbors
9:30 a.m.	Welcome by the City Manager Introduction of speakers
10:00 a.m.	Bob Griscom, Prairie Lane Development Company
10:15 a.m.	Loretta Swift, Save our Earth
10:30 a.m.	Questions from the floor

16 Who should attend the meeting?

    (A) Residents on Manchester Boulevard
    (B) Out-of-state tourists
    (C) A building contractor
    (D) All the community members

17 What will probably happen at the meeting?

    (A) One invited speaker will make a presentation.
    (B) City leaders will decide how many buildings to allow.
    (C) Presenters will give different points of view.
    (D) All new building will be prohibited.

18 When will the city leaders consider development?

    (A) They will decide at 9:00 a.m. on Saturday.
    (B) They have already decided.
    (C) In the next thirty days or so.
    (D) Immediately after the meeting.

19 Why should the local residents go to the meeting?

    (A) For breakfast and to meet their neighbors
    (B) To join an environmental group
    (C) To elect officials
    (D) To help decide the future of their community

20 What changes to the meeting are announced in the flyer?

    (A) Speakers
    (B) Topic
    (C) Time
    (D) Location

Reading

Part 7				
16	Ⓐ	Ⓑ	Ⓒ	Ⓓ
17	Ⓐ	Ⓑ	Ⓒ	Ⓓ
18	Ⓐ	Ⓑ	Ⓒ	Ⓓ
19	Ⓐ	Ⓑ	Ⓒ	Ⓓ
20	Ⓐ	Ⓑ	Ⓒ	Ⓓ

Listening PART 1

Strategy A

Use the pictures to identify a situation. Ask yourself *who* is doing *what*, *where*.

Who?	The officer is on the bridge of the ship.
What?	He's looking through binoculars.
Where?	The ship is heading out to sea.

Who?	The passenger is being served by the flight attendant.
What?	The flight attendant is offering the passenger some refreshments.
Where?	The passenger is sitting on the aisle.

Task A

Identify a situation

Match the ends of the sentences (A–E) with the beginnings (1–5) to make a situation.

1 The airline sales agent behind the counter ....

(A) find their cabin on B Deck.

2 The pilot is checking the instruments ....

(B) loading goods onto the ship.

3 The purser is helping the passengers ....

(C) is validating the ticket.

4 The porter is carrying ....

(D) in the cockpit before takeoff.

5 The sailor is on the dock ....

(E) the passengers' luggage through the station.

Strategy B

Be aware of similar sounds. The TOEIC® test often uses similar sounding words to confuse you. Note the similar sounding words in these examples.

(A)	The train is in the station.	(A)	They're being weighed today.
(B)	The pants are on the hanger.	(B)	They're waiting for a train.
(C)	The plane is in the hangar.	(C)	They're walking in the rain.
(D)	The playing lane is narrow.	(D)	They're loading grain.

The correct answer is (C).   The correct answer is (B).

Task B 🎧

Identify the correct word

Listen to the pairs of sentences. Mark *1* beside the word you hear in the first sentence, and *2* beside the word you hear in the second sentence.

6 purse ....
   purser ....

7 musicians ....
   magicians ....

8 cars ....
   carts ....

9 thanked her ....
   tanker ....

10 let her ....
    letter ....

Review 🎧

Directions: Listen and select the one statement that best describes what you see in the picture.

11

12

13

14

Listening

Part 1				
11	Ⓐ	Ⓑ	Ⓒ	Ⓓ
12	Ⓐ	Ⓑ	Ⓒ	Ⓓ
13	Ⓐ	Ⓑ	Ⓒ	Ⓓ
14	Ⓐ	Ⓑ	Ⓒ	Ⓓ

PART 2

Strategy A

Listen for questions beginning with *what time*, *when* and *how (often)* for indications of time.

> *What time* does the train depart?
> *When* will the plane arrive?
> *How long* does it take to get from here to your office?
> *How frequently* does the express train run?
> *How often* are there non-stop flights?
> *How much time* do I need to get to the airport?
> *How soon* will lunch be served?

Task A

Identify time

Underline the words that indicate time in the questions. Cross out the answer choice that is NOT possible.

1   How frequently does the freighter call at this port?

   (A)   About six times a year.
   (B)   ~~Any day now.~~
   (C)   Only twice a month.

2   When will the cabin attendants clean the cabin?

   (A)   They usually do it right after breakfast.
   (B)   When they are old enough.
   (C)   Whenever you want.

3   What time does the gate agent expect the flight to depart?

   (A)   At 5:15.
   (B)   As soon as the flight crew boards.
   (C)   On daylight saving time.

4   How many minutes more until we land?

   (A)   About ten.
   (B)   There are sixty in an hour.
   (C)   We should be on the ground in a few minutes.

5   How late do you expect the train to be?

   (A)   Earlier.
   (B)   Only a few minutes behind schedule.
   (C)   It won't be here for another hour at least.

6   How long will we have to wait for a taxi?

   (A)   In this rain, forever.
   (B)   More than a few minutes.
   (C)   I waited an hour for you.

7   On what days are there direct flights to Rio?

   (A)   Every day but Monday
   (B)   Any day now
   (C)   Only on Wednesdays

8   When do you think the fares will increase?

   (A)   At the end of this quarter.
   (B)   I think it is very expensive.
   (C)   They usually raise the prices every June.

9   How much longer will it take them to fuel the plane?

   (A)   Just a few more minutes.
   (B)   They should finish in a half an hour.
   (C)   It's a long time to go without fuel.

10   How often do passenger ships dock here?

   (A)   They rarely come here anymore.
   (B)   You see them here daily.
   (C)   At 4 in the afternoon.

Real Spoken English

How soon till we land?
This is the common spoken form of *How soon is it until we land?*
What about taking an earlier train?
This is the common spoken form of *Why don't we take a train that leaves earlier?*

Strategy B

Listen for time markers in *yes/no* questions.
A time marker is any word that helps you determine when an action occurs.

> The plane is *always* on time, isn't it?
> Can you tell me *when* the movie *begins*?
> Do you think that the flight will be *late*?
> Have the other flights been canceled *yet*?
> You were supposed to *leave a week ago*, weren't you?
> Is it possible to *finish* this *today*?
> Your cruise took *longer* than you thought, didn't it?
> I suppose they'll serve *dinner* on your flight, won't they?

Task B

Identify time markers in *yes / no* questions

Cross out the answer choice that is NOT possible. Then underline the time markers in the two possible answer choices.

11　Could you tell me when dinner is served?

　　(A)　In about <u>five minutes</u>.
　　(B)　~~In the main dining room.~~
　　(C)　At <u>7 p.m.</u>

12　Freighters are often behind schedule, aren't they?

　　(A)　Yes, there are always delays on the trips.
　　(B)　No, the schedule is in the front of the book.
　　(C)　Yes, and a delay of one day is very costly.

13　If you don't leave soon, you'll miss your plane, won't you?

　　(A)　I didn't realize how much I missed them.
　　(B)　We need to leave now to get there on time.
　　(C)　No, I allowed plenty of time.

14　Do you think they'll serve breakfast before landing?

　　(A)　Yes, at 7 in the morning, about an hour before we touch down.
　　(B)　I just have coffee for breakfast.
　　(C)　No. Since we don't get in until noon, I think they'll serve lunch.

15　Wouldn't it be quicker to take the 8:15 train?

　　(A)　It would be, but the 9:00 has a dining car.
　　(B)　Yes, the early morning express is always faster.
　　(C)　I tried to be quick, but I missed the train.

Review 🎧

Directions: Listen and select the best response to the question or statement.

Listening			
Part 2			
16	Ⓐ	Ⓑ	Ⓒ
17	Ⓐ	Ⓑ	Ⓒ
18	Ⓐ	Ⓑ	Ⓒ
19	Ⓐ	Ⓑ	Ⓒ
20	Ⓐ	Ⓑ	Ⓒ
21	Ⓐ	Ⓑ	Ⓒ
22	Ⓐ	Ⓑ	Ⓒ
23	Ⓐ	Ⓑ	Ⓒ
24	Ⓐ	Ⓑ	Ⓒ
25	Ⓐ	Ⓑ	Ⓒ

PART 3

Strategy A

Use the questions and answers to guess the topic of conversation. Look for questions that begin with *what*.

> *What* is the problem?
> *What* is the conversation about?
> *What* are they discussing?

Task A

Identify the topic of conversation

Match the parts of the conversation to the appropriate answer choices.

1   What is the problem?

   (A) Mr. Park's ticket is missing.
   (B) Mr. Park is late for his flight.
   (C) The road to the airport is closed.
   (D) The taxi hasn't arrived.

I can't seem to remember where I put my ticket. ...*A*......
The cab should have been here ten minutes ago. ....
The traffic report said it was impossible to drive to the airport. ....
If I don't get to the gate in two minutes, they'll close the door. ....

> **Test Note**
> *What is the problem?* is a very common question on Part 3 of the TOEIC test.

2   What is the conversation about?

   (A) A late departure
   (B) A sick crew member
   (C) A turbulent ride
   (D) A missed connection

Our flight was canceled because one of the flight attendants became ill. ....
I only had ten minutes to get from one gate to the next, and by the time I got there, they had closed the door. ....
The captain requests that you remain in your seat with your seatbelts fastened. ....
Because of the weather, our flight will not leave as scheduled. ....

3   What are they discussing?

   (A) Mechanical failure
   (B) A shortage of technicians
   (C) A potential strike
   (D) Worker benefits

If the union demands aren't met, they will stop work. ....
It is difficult to find skilled and experienced workers to repair the electrical components in these cars. ....
All trains are delayed because of a problem with several engines. ....
The union employees gained increased health care and vacation days with the last contract. ....

4   What is the topic of discussion?

   (A) Trains being late
   (B) A prerequisite for departure
   (C) An airport arrival
   (D) The use of public transportation

He's probably coming on the next flight. ....
Snow on the tracks is the number one reason for delays in winter. ....
Mass transit in this city serves about 20% of commuters on a regular basis. ....
The ship can't sail until the engineer has arrived. ....

5   What is the problem?

   (A) The bus is crowded.
   (B) The passenger missed her stop.
   (C) The driver couldn't make change.
   (D) The rain was coming in the windows.

I'm sorry. You need the exact change on this bus. ....
Move to the rear of the bus. Make room for boarding passengers. ....
Driver! Driver! Stop the bus! Stop! I was supposed to get off. ....
Shut the windows! The seats will get wet. ....

Strategy B

Use the questions and answer choices to limit the possible reasons for an action.
Pay attention to questions that begin with *why*.

Why is the hotel guest complaining?
Why has the tourist not unpacked her bags?
Why did the president not make the plane?

Task B

Identify the reason for an action

Read a line from a conversation. Then underline the answer choice that correctly identifies the reason.

6   "Marcia should take a book to read since the flight is long."
    Why should she take a book along?

    (A)   To pass the time.
    (B)   Because it's a best-seller.
    (C)   To make people think she is intelligent.
    (D)   She needs to write a book report.

7   "Mr. Sim is taking the train to Rome because he doesn't like to fly."
    Why is Mr. Sim taking the train?

    (A)   He enjoys watching the Italian scenery.
    (B)   The journey to Rome is too short to fly.
    (C)   He prefers not to fly.
    (D)   The plane was overbooked.

8   "Since I may not like the room, don't bring the bags until I check it out."
    Why doesn't the speaker want the bags brought to the room now?

    (A)   He's going to check out of the hotel.
    (B)   He wants to look the room over first.
    (C)   He wants to carry them himself.
    (D)   He's going to put them in storage.

9   "The constant motion of a ship makes me ill, so I've never taken a cruise."
    Why doesn't the speaker take a cruise?

    (A)   He doesn't like the constant activity.
    (B)   He has been in the hospital.
    (C)   He gets seasick.
    (D)   He can't afford it.

Review 🎧

Directions: Listen and select the best response to each question.

10   What is the problem?
    (A)   The plane is late.
    (B)   There are a lot of people in line.
    (C)   The man missed his flight.
    (D)   There are too many ticket agents.

11   Why doesn't the man go directly to the gate?
    (A)   He is waiting to check his bags.
    (B)   He needs to buy a ticket.
    (C)   He missed his flight.
    (D)   He doesn't have any luggage.

12   Why does the woman have to wait?
    (A) Her flight is delayed.
    (B) She doesn't have a ticket.
    (C) Her carry-on bag is too large.
    (D) She's traveling with a group.

13   Why can't the woman check in to her room?
    (A)   It's only 3 o'clock.
    (B)   The room is being made up now.
    (C)   Check-in time is at 12 o'clock.
    (D)   She doesn't have a reservation.

14   What is the reason for the problem?
    (A)   She didn't want a suite.
    (B)   People waited in the lobby.
    (C)   Guests did not leave before noon.
    (D)   Her friends were late.

15   Why does the woman decline the clerk's offer?
    (A)   She is expecting to meet some people soon.
    (B)   She doesn't want to stay in a suite.
    (C)   She checked out late.
    (D)   She wants a more comfortable room.

Listening			
Part 3			
10	Ⓐ Ⓑ Ⓒ Ⓓ		
11	Ⓐ Ⓑ Ⓒ Ⓓ		
12	Ⓐ Ⓑ Ⓒ Ⓓ		
13	Ⓐ Ⓑ Ⓒ Ⓓ		
14	Ⓐ Ⓑ Ⓒ Ⓓ		
15	Ⓐ Ⓑ Ⓒ Ⓓ		

PART 4

Task A 🎧

Identify speaker and target listeners

You will hear three talks. Before each talk begins, read the answer choices quickly. Then listen and select the best answer.

1   Who is talking?

   (A) A pilot
   (B) A flight attendant
   (C) A gate agent
   (D) A first class passenger

2   Who is most likely listening to the announcement?

   (A) Only frequent flyers
   (B) The cabin crew
   (C) The ground staff
   (D) All passengers

3   Who is talking?

   (A) A purser
   (B) A travel agent
   (C) A sailor
   (D) A social director

4   Who is most likely listening to the advertisement?

   (A) Potential travelers
   (B) Novice sailors
   (C) Musicians
   (D) Hotel staff

5   Who is most likely talking?

   (A) A tour guide
   (B) A shopper from New York
   (C) A shopkeeper
   (D) A citizen of New Jersey

6   Who is most likely listening to the announcement?

   (A) Tourists
   (B) Actresses
   (C) Luxury store owners
   (D) Tour guides

Strategy B

Use the questions and answers to focus on numbers in quantities, times, and amounts. Before the talks begin, read the questions and the answer choices quickly. Pay attention to questions that begin with *when* and *how*.

> *When* did he arrive?
> *When* was the timetable published?
> *How long* will the flight last?
> *How much* does the ticket cost?

Task B

Identify quantity and amount

Cross out the sentence that does NOT have the same meaning as the other two.

7   We need at least a dozen towels.
    I asked for a couple of towels.
    Don't give us less than twelve.

8   She'll be staying at the hotel for two weeks.
    Her reservation is for fourteen days.
    She'll check out in five-business days.

9   I need this in less than 24 hours – no later than noon.
    Is it possible to have it ready by 12:00 tomorrow?
    Anytime after dinner is fine.

10 All of the tickets cost $10.
    He bought ten tickets which cost $100 each.
    He spent $1000 on tickets.

Review 🎧

Directions: Listen and select the best response to each question.

11 Who is speaking?
    (A) An army captain
    (B) An airline captain
    (C) A sea captain
    (D) A restaurant captain

12 When will the plane land?
    (A) In 10 minutes
    (B) In 20 minutes
    (C) In 30 minutes
    (D) In 70 minutes

13 Why should the crew take their seats?
    (A) The plane will land in twenty minutes.
    (B) The weather is turbulent.
    (C) They need to help the pilot.
    (D) They're in training.

_____

14 Who is listening to this speech?
    (A) Hotel guests
    (B) Banquet caterers
    (C) Hotel executives
    (D) Industrial workers

15 What was the average hotel occupancy rate?
    (A) 40%
    (B) 60%
    (C) 80%
    (D) 100%

16 Who is making the toast?
    (A) A hotel guest
    (B) A hotel manager
    (C) A room clerk
    (D) A travel agent

Listening			
Part 4			
11	Ⓐ Ⓑ Ⓒ Ⓓ		
12	Ⓐ Ⓑ Ⓒ Ⓓ		
13	Ⓐ Ⓑ Ⓒ Ⓓ		
14	Ⓐ Ⓑ Ⓒ Ⓓ		
15	Ⓐ Ⓑ Ⓒ Ⓓ		
16	Ⓐ Ⓑ Ⓒ Ⓓ		

Reading PART 5

Strategy A

Look at the words around the blank and focus on their grammatical forms to determine the missing part of speech.

> When the price of oil rises, the price of air tickets ....
> (A) increases (C) increasing
> (B) increased (D) increasingly

When	the	price	of	oil	rises,	the	price	of	air tickets	....
conj.	det.	noun	prep	noun	verb	det.	noun	prep	noun	verb

Choice (A) *increases* can be a noun or verb.
Choice (B) *increased* can be a verb or a participle.
Choice (C) *increasing* is a participle.
Choice (D) *increasingly* is an adverb.

The correct answer is (A). The main clause needs a verb. Answer choices (A) and (B) are both verbs. The verb in the sub clause is in the present simple tense and talks generally about when things happen. The main clause should also be in this tense, so the correct answer is (A).

> **Grammar Glossary** **Parts of Speech** (p115) **Word Families** (p119)

Task A

Identify the part of speech

Write the part of speech (noun, verb, adverb, adjective) for each answer choice.
Then choose the word or phrase that best completes the sentence.

1 The .... of many countries depends on tourism.

   (A) economize ....
   (B) economical ....
   (C) economically ....
   (D) economy ....

2 The hotel director .... a large staff.

   (A) management ....
   (B) manager ....
   (C) manages ....
   (D) managerial ....

3 When .... airlines are privatized, service usually improves.

   (A) national ....
   (B) nation ....
   (C) nationality ....
   (D) nationalize ....

4 If you express yourself .... , it will be easier for people to understand you.

   (A) simple ....
   (B) simplification ....
   (C) simplify ....
   (D) simply ....

5 Museums are visited more often by tourists than ....

   (A) location ....
   (B) locate ....
   (C) locals ....
   (D) localize ....

6 Package .... are extremely popular with elderly and single travelers.

   (A) tourism ....
   (B) toured ....
   (C) tourists ....
   (D) tours ....

Strategy B

Look for passive verb markers to complete a prepositional phrase.
An active verb is changed into a passive one by changing the active verb into the past participle form and putting a form of the verb *to be* in front of it. The preposition *by* usually follows. These are both indications that the verb is a passive verb.

Active: An experienced guide gave the tour.
Passive: The tour *was given by* an experienced guide.

Grammar Glossary   **Verbs: Active/Passive   (p117)**

Task B

Identify the appropriate preposition

Underline the correct preposition. Then mark *P* if the verb is passive or *A* if it is active.

7   The brochure was written *by / to* an experienced travel agent. ....

8   The translator wrote *by / to* the editor. ....

9   The room was cleaned *by / upon* the head housekeeper. ....

10   The maintenance crew cleaned the aircraft *by / upon* arrival. ....

11   The train doesn't stop *by / at* every station during rush hour. ....

Review

Directions: Select the best response to complete the sentence.

12 Airline policies .... the amount of carry-on luggage.

- (A) limit
- (B) limitation
- (C) limitless
- (D) limiting

13 This ticket needs to be endorsed .... the issuing agent.

- (A) on
- (B) with
- (C) by
- (D) at

14 The flight attendant gave a safety .... before take off.

- (A) demonstrator
- (B) demonstration
- (C) demonstrate
- (D) demonstrable

15 Large bags must be checked .... airline personnel.

- (A) from
- (B) to
- (C) toward
- (D) by

16 The tour guide .... the sites she would show us.

- (A) described
- (B) description
- (C) describable
- (D) describing

Reading
Part 5
12 Ⓐ Ⓑ Ⓒ Ⓓ
13 Ⓐ Ⓑ Ⓒ Ⓓ
14 Ⓐ Ⓑ Ⓒ Ⓓ
15 Ⓐ Ⓑ Ⓒ Ⓓ
16 Ⓐ Ⓑ Ⓒ Ⓓ

PART 6

Strategy A

Read the sentence quickly to yourself to see if the verb + preposition combination "sounds right". This section of the TOEIC test is the place to trust your ear. If something "sounds wrong", look carefully at the preposition and try replacing it with others. The verb and preposition not only need to sound right together, but also to have the right meaning for the context.

Look at the difference:

> The plane *took off* at 5:35.
> A new travel agent *took over* my account.
> The flight attendant *took away* the food tray.

Each of the three sentences is correct. They all use the same verb but with a different preposition in each sentence. This changes the meaning of the verb each time.

Grammar Glossary **Verbs + Prepositions** (p118)

Task A

Identify the verb + preposition combinations

Match each verb with all of its possible prepositions. Then write the correct verb + preposition in the sentences.

out of up on down

count *out, count up, count on, count down* ....

check ....

cut ....

work ....

take care ....

1   To reduce costs, the airlines have .... serving food on short flights.

2   To keep fit, pilots .... in the gym at least three times a week.

3   The gate agents .... passengers who need special assistance.

4   Travelers .... a clean room when they check into a hotel.

5   The housekeeping manager .... her staff while they work.

Strategy B

The verb of a sentence must match the subject in number. It must be either singular or plural. On the TOEIC test many words, phrases, or clauses often separate the subject from its verb. Look carefully for the subject.

The messenger service used by all our departments .... before noon.
- (A) come
- (B) comes
- (C) coming
- (D) has come

(B) is the correct answer. The subject of the sentence is *service*, which is singular, so the verb must also be singular. Do not be confused by words which separate the subject from the verb. Here *departments* is plural and is close to the verb, but it is not the subject of the sentence.

> **Grammar Glossary** **Subject and Verbs of a Sentence** (p117)
> **Verb Agreement** (p118)

Task B

Identify subject/verb agreement

Underline the subjects below and mark *S* for a singular subject, *NC* for non-count or *P* for plural. Write the correct form of the verb if it is incorrect.

6 <u>A cruise</u> [S] aboard the new *Titanic* or its sister ship *Grand* are [is] available at bargain prices now.

7 Seats on all of our flights, including the coach-only flight to Madrid, is assigned on the day of departure.

8 The itinerary given to all travelers was a four-city trip in five days.

9 The Travel Association's annual business travel forecast predict overall travel costs jumping 5% next year.

10 Once luggage are checked at the ticket counter, it is routed through a high-tech security scanner.

11 The hotel, one of the newest in the chain, is located a mile south of the airport and include a golf-course on the grounds.

12 Disembarking from the plane to a waiting bus is not as convenient as walking off the plane using a jet way.

13 The restaurants located on boats in the harbor and the new restaurant on the dock specializes in seafood.

14 Most of the city's major business hotels line avenues parallel to the beach.

15 Airlines, which compete to provide the best service, offers amenities like a personal video at every seat.

Review

Directions: Select the best answer to complete the text.

Questions 16–19 refer to the following letter.

Hodgeson and Partners • 3399 West Newton Lane • Brookline, MA 02146

Serge LaRoche, Manager
Easy Executive Travel
4233 Lincoln Road, STE 438
Barnesville, MD 20838

Dear Mr. LaRoche:

I want to thank you and your staff for your assistance in planning our Sales and Marketing Conference, which was held at the Wani Wani Resort last weekend. Special commendation goes to your agents who _____ to help us by preparing a detailed summary of the arrangements.

    16   (A) continue
          (B) continues
          (C) continuing
          (D) to continue

One of your agents _____ a place in "travel agent heaven." Mr. Marco Rossini was able to change

        17   (A) deserve
              (B) deserves
              (C) deserving
              (D) to deserve

flight arrangements, car rentals, and hotel accommodations at the last minute. He was always polite, efficient, and calm. Our attendees all remarked on the extraordinary care that he took to make sure all of our needs were taken care _____.

            18   (A) with
                  (B) on
                  (C) in
                  (D) of

Your agency has earned our respect and our future business. We look _____ to working with you

                19   (A) on
                      (B) at
                      (C) forward
                      (D) back

in the near future.

Sincerely,

Bob Wilson

Bob Wilson
Event Coordinator

Reading				
Part 6				
16	Ⓐ	Ⓑ	Ⓒ	Ⓓ
17	Ⓐ	Ⓑ	Ⓒ	Ⓓ
18	Ⓐ	Ⓑ	Ⓒ	Ⓓ
19	Ⓐ	Ⓑ	Ⓒ	Ⓓ

PART 7

What type of clothing may NOT be worn in the lobby?
(A) Swim attire
(B) Golf shoes
(C) Running outfits
(D) Bathrobes

Notice

Our guests are kindly requested not to run in the pool area or to wear golf shoes on the rubber mat surrounding the pool. We ask that guests crossing the lobby from the swimming pool wear cover-up garments like a bathrobe.

(A) is the correct answer.

In the question above there are keywords that answer *what* and *where*. *What* is the *type of clothing* and *where* is *the lobby*. Your task is to identify the article of clothing that can NOT be worn in the lobby.

Read the notice quickly and look for the four answer choices. The verb *run* and the noun phrase *golf shoes* are found, but they are associated with the pool area not the lobby. So you can eliminate (B) and (C). Only (A) *swim attire* (swim suits) and (D) *bathrobes* are associated with the lobby. A quick reading indicates that hotel guests should conceal their swimsuits, that is they should hide them and NOT let them be seen in the lobby. Therefore (D) is not the correct answer as bathrobes are allowed to be worn in the lobby. This leaves (A).

Task A

Identify restrictions

Cross out the answer choices that are NOT related to the main underlined topic.

1   <u>Patio furniture</u> is NOT to be removed.

    (A)   ~~Trees~~
    (B)   Chairs
    (C)   Seat cushions
    (D)   ~~Medicine cabinets~~

2   In case of <u>emergency</u>, locate the exit nearest you.

    (A)   Earthquake
    (B)   Fire
    (C)   Fatigue
    (D)   Flooding

3   <u>Disabled passengers or passengers needing special accommodation</u> are invited to board at this time.

    (A)   Passengers in wheelchairs
    (B)   Passengers with first-class tickets
    (C)   Elderly passengers
    (D)   Passengers with small children

4   <u>Change is NOT given without purchase.</u>

    (A)   I can only get small coins if I buy something.
    (B)   I can only use small coins to buy something.
    (C)   When I buy something, I can get some single bills or coins.
    (D)   I cannot exchange anything I buy.

Strategy B

Read the answer choices and text quickly to look for time markers.
As you learn to look for specific answers to specific questions, you will learn to avoid irrelevant information.

At what time of day are there the most flights?
(A) Early in the morning
(B) At noon
(C) Mid-afternoon
(D) Late evening

Flight Schedule from Antwerp		
0600	AF3200	Paris
0600	SQ 1	Singapore
0610	KG 342	Frankfurt
0630	LH 452	Strutgart
0635	BA 818	London
1215	AF 1627	Lille
1230	LH 334	Berlin
1315	BA 819	London
1530	AF 1440	Paris
1540	TY 234	Istanbul
1850	BA 820	London
2000	LH 56	Munich

(A) is the correct answer. The key words *what time* indicate that you are to locate *when*. The key words *most flights* tell you *what*.

Before you read the passage, you should quickly translate the answer choices into time blocks.

Choice (A) *Early in the morning* is between 5:00 a.m. and 9:00 a.m. approximately.

Choice (B) *At noon* is around twelve o'clock.

Choice (C) *Mid-afternoon* is between 2:30 p.m. and 4:00 p.m.

Choice (D) *Late evening* is after 10:00 p.m.

A quick scan of the schedule shows that the most flights leave between 0600 and 0635 in fact almost 50% of the flights leave at that time. Therefore, the correct answer is (A), *Early in the morning*.

Task B

Identify time

Match the time markers (A–F) with their approximate equivalents (5–10).

5	in a week	(A)	daily
6	biannually	(B)	twice a year
7	every two weeks	(C)	in two days' time
8	every day	(D)	within seven days
9	an hour and a half	(E)	90 minutes
10	the day after tomorrow	(F)	fortnightly

Strategy C

One of the questions in the double passage set may ask you to identify a location. Read the questions and answer choices quickly. Look for questions about location and decide if you will need information from both passages to answer the question. These questions usually begin with *where*. They may also contain prepositions of place, such as *from*, *at*, *to* or measures of distance, such as *how far*, *how close*, etc.

1 Where is flight 002's new gate in relation to the original gate?
   (A) A long walk to a different terminal
   (B) A short walk to a different concourse
   (C) A very short walk to the new gate
   (D) Too far to walk

JAL 002 LAX to NRT boards Terminal 1, Gate A-12, 12:45 p.m. Check monitor at airport for last minute changes.

Flight	Destination	Concourse/Gate	Time	Comments
AA16	Osaka	A-12	11:55	Gate change
H4342	Mexico City	C-14	12:15	On time
BA33	London	C-41	12:30	Delayed
JAL002	Tokyo	A-14	12:45	Gate change
NW60	Seoul	A-31	12:45	Canceled

(C) is the correct answer. The airport monitor shows that the new gate is A-14, which will be very close to A-12. (A) The airport monitor does not indicate that the new gate is at a different terminal. (B) Both gates are at the same concourse, A. (D) This option is not suggested by the information given.

Task C

Identify location

Write the answer to the location question.

11 You may wonder how I ended up in Malaysia. Before I came to the United States, I studied in Peru. After I graduated from college in the US, I got my first job in Tokyo. This led me to Hong Kong, Singapore, and finally to my present job.

Where am I now? ....

12 The travel agency meant to send the tickets by overnight mail, but they came by regular mail instead. Consequently, the tickets only arrived yesterday. I put them in my desk drawer, but my secretary thought we should put them in the office safe. On the way there, she stopped for coffee in the cafeteria and absent-mindedly left them on a table. The cleaning staff found them and gave them to the security guard, who put them on my desk.

Where did the traveler put his tickets?

....

13 I never thought I would stay in my hometown. I wanted to travel and see the world. I wanted to visit Paris and Rome. I wanted to take a boat to China and a train across Russia. I wanted to ride horseback across Mongolia. Instead, I'm still here walking across the same street I've walked across since I was a child.

Where is this person now?

....

14 This is your pilot speaking. We are going to make a slight detour. Our flight path today was to take us from New York over the polar route to Stockholm. However, there is a bad weather ahead so it will be a more comfortable ride if we take the longer route straight across the Atlantic. We will arrive in Sweden later than anticipated, but we will travel in comfort.

Which route is the pilot going to take?

....

Review

Directions: Read the information and select the best answer for each question.

Questions 15–19 refer to the following policy statement and email.

To ensure that your reservation on China Air is not canceled, you must check-in for all domestic flights one hour before boarding time. You must be at the departure gate twenty minutes before boarding time. For international flights, you must check in at least two hours before boarding time. You must be at the departure gate thirty minutes before boarding time.

Travelers to Hong Kong or Macao must check in 90 minutes before boarding time.

All international travelers are required to reconfirm their flight at least 72 hours prior to departure. Flights to Hong Kong or Macao do not require reconfirmation.

To:	China Air Customer Service
From:	Kent Karlock
Sub:	Denied boarding

I want to register a complaint. I had a first class ticket on China Air 8712 to Macao for December 8. The flight departed at 5:15. I was at the airport by 4:30 and had plenty of time to get to the gate. Please explain why your agents refused to honor my ticket.

15 When must domestic travelers report to the departure gate?

    (A) Immediately after checking in
    (B) 20 minutes before boarding
    (C) A half hour before boarding
    (D) Before checking in

16 Why did Mr. Karlock not fly China Air 8712?

    (A) He had not paid for his ticket.
    (B) He arrived too late to check in.
    (C) He complained too much.
    (D) First class was full.

17 How many minutes before departure should international travelers check-in?

    (A) 20
    (B) 30
    (C) 90
    (D) 120

18 Which travelers must confirm three days in advance to ensure their reservations?

    (A) International travelers
    (B) Domestic travelers
    (C) Travelers to Macao or Hong Kong
    (D) All travelers follow the same procedure

19 "Honor" in the last line of the email is closest in meaning to

    (A) refund
    (B) accept
    (C) reward
    (D) praise

Reading

Part 7				
15	Ⓐ	Ⓑ	Ⓒ	Ⓓ
16	Ⓐ	Ⓑ	Ⓒ	Ⓓ
17	Ⓐ	Ⓑ	Ⓒ	Ⓓ
18	Ⓐ	Ⓑ	Ⓒ	Ⓓ
19	Ⓐ	Ⓑ	Ⓒ	Ⓓ

Chapter 5 Technical Areas

Listening PART 1

Strategy A

Use the pictures to determine specific details. The TOEIC® test often uses statements that seem to be correct. These statements describe the picture generally, but yet are wrong about a specific detail. Ask yourself *where* to determine the general context and the specific context.

General Context
The man is in the control room.

Specific Details
The engineer is looking at the controls on the right.
The chair is on wheels.

General Context
The woman is in the laboratory.

Specific Details
The technician is looking through the microscope.
There are flasks and bottles in front of the woman.

Task A

Identify the specific details

Write the letters of two specific details that match the general context.

General Context

1   The computer is in a room.   .... *A* .... *F*

2   The people are in the studio.   ....

3   He's standing by the machine.   ....

4   The drawings are on the wall.   ....

5   She's pouring liquid.   ....

Specific Details
(A)   The laptop computer is in the manager's office.
(B)   The diagrams are taped to the wall.
(C)   A man is unpacking the fax machine.
(D)   The sound technicians are checking the microphones.
(E)   The researcher is adding liquid to a beaker.
(F)   The computer's monitor is on a shelf.
(G)   The musicians are getting ready to record.
(H)   The office technician is opening a box.
(I)   The laboratory assistant is holding a beaker.
(J)   They are diagrams of electrical circuit boards.

Strategy B

Be aware of homophones and homonyms.
The TOEIC test often uses words that sound the same but have different meanings. This is done to distract you from the correct answer. Look at these words in these examples.

(A)   The crane's lifting a steel <u>bar</u>.
(B)   They're working in a <u>bar</u>.

The correct answer is (A).

(A)   The windmills are on the <u>plain</u>.
(B)   The propellers are on the <u>plane</u>.

The correct answer is (A).

Task B 🎧

Identify the similar sounding words

Read sentence 6, then listen to two sentences. Mark *A* or *B* to indicate the sentence that is related to the sentence you read. Continue with sentences 7–10.

	A / B	homophone / homonym
6	....*B*.... The motor made an unusual noise when we turned it on.	............*belt*............
7	.... The computer room was filled with the new trainees.	....
8	.... Over fifty microscopes were installed in the laboratory.	....
9	.... When we moved the ladder, we knocked over the toolbox.	....
10	.... All of the wires from the appliances created a fire hazard.	....

Now listen again and write the homophone or homonym that you hear in each of the two sentences.

Review 🎧

Directions: Listen and select the one statement that best describes what you see in the picture.

11

12

13

14

Listening

	Part 1			
11	Ⓐ	Ⓑ	Ⓒ	Ⓓ
12	Ⓐ	Ⓑ	Ⓒ	Ⓓ
13	Ⓐ	Ⓑ	Ⓒ	Ⓓ
14	Ⓐ	Ⓑ	Ⓒ	Ⓓ

PART 2

Strategy A

Listen for question words that ask for a reason. Questions that ask for a reason usually begin with *why*. The reason itself may begin with *because*, or a reason may be stated without the need of *because*.

Why did you buy that type of calculator?
Because it can perform a number of functions.

Why didn't you attend the neuroscience conference?
I was in the middle of some experiments and I didn't have the time.

Task A

Identify the possible reason

Cross out the answer choices that are NOT possible.

1 Why did you buy new appliances?
(A) At the store on the corner near the school and the hospital.
(B) They use a different voltage system.
(C) I don't think the old ones will work in Brazil.

2 Why are the utility crews in the intersection?
(A) The men in the orange jackets.
(B) They're doing an annual inspection.
(C) One of the water mains broke.

3 Why does it take so long to fuel the airplane?
(A) Jets use so much fuel that it has to be stored in the wings.
(B) Because the tanks are already full.
(C) Fuel is added slowly and carefully.

4 Why did they take the machine apart?
(A) The tools are right there.
(B) Someone spilled coffee on it.
(C) There seemed to be a short in the connections.

5 Why does the company continue to use Good Earth's landscaping?
(A) We couldn't have made a smarter move.
(B) Their rates are more competitive.
(C) The owner is a friend of the president.

6 Why did the new engineer disassemble all of the machines?
(A) To find the defective parts.
(B) It was the fifth time the machines were returned.
(C) It was the only way to solve the problem.

7 Why is the research and development office closing?
(A) An article about their research was published recently.
(B) They've added more staff.
(C) R & D is no longer being funded.

8 Why are they reducing the technical service staff?
(A) The volume of calls has dropped dramatically in the last year.
(B) The company has contracted with an outside company to handle the problems.
(C) I don't care how long I have to wait if they can fix it.

9 Why haven't they released the latest version of the computer operating system?
(A) The computer has many new programs installed.
(B) They wanted to wait until they could fix the bugs.
(C) No, they haven't been on display.

10 Why are all of the containers still on the dock?
(A) The workers went on strike last night.
(B) There was an electrical malfunction with the cranes.
(C) There are over 50 shipments from China sitting on the deck.

Strategy B

To identify opinion questions, add "*What do you think?*" Then listen for answer choices that show what the speaker thinks.

> *Should we hire the recent college graduate?*

You can easily add "What do you think, should we hire the college graduate?" and identify that the question is asking for an opinion. The answer choice should indicate an opinion, not a fact.

Real Spoken English
In common speech, we often voice our opinions by starting with:

In my opinion …
or
I think …
or
I believe that …

In the TOEIC test, these clues are often omitted.

Task B

Identify the possible opinion
Cross out the answer choice that is NOT possible.

11 Can we finish the installation today?
   (A) They close in fifteen minutes.
   (B) If we hurry, we should be able to.
   (C) It's going to be difficult.

12 Will the current system be adequate for our energy needs in 10 years?
   (A) We hope that it will be.
   (B) Five years ago we changed systems.
   (C) The experts don't believe that it will be.

13 What are the results of the experiment?
   (A) We received them around an hour ago.
   (B) They turned out surprisingly well.
   (C) We're divided on how we should interpret them.

14 What do you think of the computer equipment?
   (A) It needs a lot of maintenance.
   (B) It is old and out of date.
   (C) Because it is old and inefficient.

15 Have we ordered enough cables?
   (A) Jack did his best to accurately predict the amount needed.
   (B) Definitely.
   (C) No, we didn't use any.

Review 🎧

Directions: Listen and select the best response to the question or statement.

Listening
| Part 2 |
| 16 Ⓐ Ⓑ Ⓒ |
| 17 Ⓐ Ⓑ Ⓒ |
| 18 Ⓐ Ⓑ Ⓒ |
| 19 Ⓐ Ⓑ Ⓒ |
| 20 Ⓐ Ⓑ Ⓒ |
| 21 Ⓐ Ⓑ Ⓒ |
| 22 Ⓐ Ⓑ Ⓒ |
| 23 Ⓐ Ⓑ Ⓒ |
| 24 Ⓐ Ⓑ Ⓒ |
| 25 Ⓐ Ⓑ Ⓒ |

PART 3

Grammar Glossary **Prepositional Phrases with *by*** (p116)

Task A

Identify a time

Underline the prepositions. Then check the answer choices that answer the question *when*.

1   (A) By the end of the month.
     (B) They started eight weeks ago.
     (C) Hopefully in a couple of weeks.
     (D) The inspection is in two weeks.

2   (A) She finished her degree last year.
     (B) At the end of last fall.
     (C) Right after she finished her graduate program.
     (D) Her first job was in Boston.

3   (A) They consider it a good investment.
     (B) As soon as the system's errors were fixed.
     (C) It is an immense improvement over the last project.
     (D) The prices came down on the day we arrived.

4   (A) It is due to open in a month.
     (B) During the last government's term.
     (C) It is on the border of Argentina and Brazil.
     (D) In 1988.

5   (A) The week after next.
     (B) To make sure we have the fastest equipment.
     (C) After the regional meetings.
     (D) The CEO comes from a different industry.

Strategy B

Look for questions that ask you to identify an occupation. Read the answer choices quickly. Then ask yourself the questions below about each of the occupations.

(A)   Engineer
(B)   Doctor
(C)   Plumber
(D)   Carpet installer

Where does he or she work?
What does he or she do?
What kind of equipment does he or she use?

Task B 🎧

Identify the correct occupation

Listen to the conversations. Cross out the answer choices that are NOT possible.

6   What is the man's occupation?

(A)   Automechanic
(B)   Pilot
(C)   Plumber
(D)   Carpet installer

7   Who are the speakers?

(A)   Nurses
(B)   Patients
(C)   Doctors
(D)   Construction workers

8   What does the man do?

(A)   He's an air conditioning specialist.
(B)   He's a computer programmer.
(C)   He's a graphic designer.
(D)   He's a pest control expert.

9   What is the woman's job?

(A)   A TV presenter
(B)   A service representative
(C)   A customer service representative
(D)   A telephone installer

Review 🎧

Directions: Listen and select the best response to each question.

10   What is the woman's occupation?

(A)   Counselor
(B)   Mail carrier
(C)   Telephone operator
(D)   Computer specialist

11   What are the telephone hours of technical support?

(A)   6:00 a.m. to noon
(B)   6:00 a.m. to 8:00 p.m.
(C)   8:00 a.m. to 8:00 p.m.
(D)   6:00 p.m. to midnight

12   How many hours a day is a technician available on the Web?

(A)   6
(B)   7
(C)   12
(D)   24

13   In which department do these people likely work?

(A)   Shipping
(B)   Product development
(C)   Sales
(D)   Manufacturing

14   How long ago did they place the order?

(A)   A week ago
(B)   Three days ago
(C)   On Friday
(D)   On May 1

15   When does the man need the shipment?

(A)   The date is not important
(B)   Before the union meeting
(C)   By May 1
(D)   Before the factory opens

Listening			
Part 3			
10	Ⓐ Ⓑ Ⓒ Ⓓ		
11	Ⓐ Ⓑ Ⓒ Ⓓ		
12	Ⓐ Ⓑ Ⓒ Ⓓ		
13	Ⓐ Ⓑ Ⓒ Ⓓ		
14	Ⓐ Ⓑ Ⓒ Ⓓ		
15	Ⓐ Ⓑ Ⓒ Ⓓ		

PART 4

Strategy A

Use the questions and answer choices to focus on the emotions and opinions of the talk. Look for questions that begin with *how* and *what*.

How do the workers feel?
How will the engineer react?
What is the tone of the talk?

Answer choices to the questions above will include adjectives describing the people and the tone.

Task A 🎧

Identify the tone

You will hear three talks. Before each talk begins, read the answer choices quickly. Then listen and choose the best answer.

1   How do the trainees feel?

  (A) Incompetent
  (B) Nervous
  (C) Excited
  (D) Bored

2   How does ACME regard its trainees?

  (A) With pride
  (B) With suspicion
  (C) With alarm
  (D) With distrust

3   What is the speaker's mood?

  (A) Angry
  (B) Relaxed
  (C) Serious
  (D) Hesitant

4   How will the speaker react if anyone asks a question?

  (A) Happily
  (B) Friendly
  (C) Calmly
  (D) Impatiently

5   What kind of person is being addressed?

  (A) A concerned business person
  (B) A disinterested worker
  (C) An energetic banker
  (D) An indifferent consumer

6   How does the announcer want the listener to feel?

  (A) Interested
  (B) Frightened
  (C) Anxious
  (D) Depressed

Strategy B

Use the questions and answers to identify the point of view. A *point of view* is an opinion or a way of looking at something.

What does the speaker think?
What is the speaker's point of view?
What is the audience's point of view?

Task B

Identify points of view

Cross out the sentences that do NOT express a point of view.

7 (A) She is difficult to work with.
 (B) She has a ticket for the next train.
 (C) She often disagrees with her colleagues.
 (D) I think she is very opinionated.

8 (A) We have been voted the world's leader in engineering supplies for three years in a row.
 (B) They should be the leader in engineering supplies.
 (C) If they continue along the same path, the company will be the leader in engineering supplies.
 (D) In 1995, they sold more engineering supplies than any other company.

9 (A) The spare parts were ordered last week.
 (B) If we don't receive the spare parts, the assembly line may have to close.
 (C) The distributor of spare parts is very unreliable.
 (D) They determined that the skyrocketing price of parts caused five companies to go out of business.

10 (A) According to policy, any malfunctions are to be reported immediately.
 (B) I believe that the machine broke down due to overuse.
 (C) This is the fifth time that we've had to call for repairs on the machine.
 (D) The machine is in the back against the left hand wall.

Review 🎧

Directions: Listen and select the best response to each question.

11 What is the speaker's point of view?
 (A) The problem can be solved.
 (B) One person is to blame.
 (C) The early shift should stay late.
 (D) The workers should not leave.

12 What is the tone of the speaker?
 (A) Friendly
 (B) Defensive
 (C) Concerned
 (D) Terrified

13 What has been the attitude of the workers?
 (A) Conscientious
 (B) Careless
 (C) Reliable
 (D) Diligent

_____

14 According to the speaker, what is most important?
 (A) Customer reaction
 (B) Worker satisfaction
 (C) Cost-cutting measures
 (D) Suppliers' deadlines

15 How does the speaker feel?
 (A) Unconcerned
 (B) Realistic
 (C) Desperate
 (D) Angry

16 What has been the customers' opinion of this business?
 (A) They refuse to do business here.
 (B) They're worried about a decline in quality.
 (C) They're satisfied with the service.
 (D) They're angry about the high prices.

Listening			
Part 4			
11	Ⓐ Ⓑ Ⓒ Ⓓ		
12	Ⓐ Ⓑ Ⓒ Ⓓ		
13	Ⓐ Ⓑ Ⓒ Ⓓ		
14	Ⓐ Ⓑ Ⓒ Ⓓ		
15	Ⓐ Ⓑ Ⓒ Ⓓ		
16	Ⓐ Ⓑ Ⓒ Ⓓ		

Reading PART 5

Strategy A

To check the subject/verb agreement ask yourself these questions:
Is the subject singular or plural?
Is it a count or non-count noun?
Is the correct form of the verb used?

The equipment .... more than fifteen containers and will cost us a fortune to send.
(A) are filling
(B) fills
(C) fill
(D) filling

Equipment is a non-count noun and therefore should take the third person singular ending "s". Therefore, you should choose answer choice (B).

> **Grammar Glossary Nouns: Count/Non-count (p114)**
> **Nouns: Singular/Plural (p114)**

Task A

Identify count and non-count nouns

Underline the nouns that the verbs refer to. Mark *C* if they are count or *NC* if they are non-count. Then choose the correct form and tense of the verbs.

The <u>scientists</u> carefully (1) ....D.... the <u>results</u> of their research which (2) ....C....
extremely valuable.

1	2
(A) guarding	(A) were
(B) guards	(B) has been
(C) are guarded	(C) are
(D) guard	(D) is

His advice, which (3) .... followed over the years, (4) .... allowed the company to succeed where many others have failed.

3	4
(A) is	(A) has
(B) were	(B) have
(C) are	(C) had
(D) was	(D) have been

Mathematics (5) .... one of the most demanding fields, yet (6) .... to draw some of the best and the brightest students.

5	6
(A) are	(A) continuing
(B) were	(B) continued
(C) am	(C) continue
(D) is	(D) continues

Strategy B

Read the sentence quickly to make sure that the meaning of the answer choice that you select is appropriate in the context of the sentence. Words that may mean the same in one context (synonyms) may not both be correct in a different context.

The foreman pulled the bell .... the end of the shift.
(A)   turning
(B)   lighting
(C)   signaling
(D)   intimating

The correct answer is (C), *signaling*. A bell cannot turn or light the end of a shift, so answer choices (A) and (B) are incorrect. Answer choice (D) looks and sounds similar to *indicate*, which is a synonym of signal, however *intimating* is incorrect.

Grammar Glossary **Synonyms** **(p117)**

Task B

Identify the synonyms

Cross out the words which are NOT synonyms of the underlined word.

7   The architects were making good progress and should be in the final planning <u>stage</u> by mid-week.

(A) phase
(B) curtain
(C) wage
(D) step

8   Technology has advanced at such a rapid <u>pace</u> that it is difficult for companies to remain current.

(A) rate
(B) tariff
(C) rhythm
(D) speed

9   The ground water had <u>seeped</u> into the pipes causing a substantial amount of damage.

(A) sipped
(B) entered
(C) slipped
(D) moved

10   Human error was a contributing <u>factor</u> to the power plant accident.

(A) reason
(B) information
(C) cause
(D) energy

11   Upon examining the circuits, they were able to identify the cause of electrical <u>malfunction</u>.

(A) failure
(B) negative
(C) breakdown
(D) efficient

Review

Directions: Choose the one word that best completes the sentence.

12 The most skilled technicians in the lab .... meeting now with the new trainees.

    (A) were
    (B) is
    (C) was
    (D) are

13 The manufacturers of the engine were unable to locate the .... part in order to fill the order.

    (A) required
    (B) obligation
    (C) necessity
    (D) retired

14 The equipment must be serviced on a .... basis, every two weeks, to maintain its efficiency.

    (A) customary
    (B) common
    (C) regular
    (D) usual

15 The sources of the information .... listed in the back of the manual.

    (A) are
    (B) isn't
    (C) aren't
    (D) is

16 The plumbers received an emergency call when the main .... broke suddenly.

    (A) pipe
    (B) jar
    (C) metal
    (D) barrel

Reading

Part 5				
12	Ⓐ	Ⓑ	Ⓒ	Ⓓ
13	Ⓐ	Ⓑ	Ⓒ	Ⓓ
14	Ⓐ	Ⓑ	Ⓒ	Ⓓ
15	Ⓐ	Ⓑ	Ⓒ	Ⓓ
16	Ⓐ	Ⓑ	Ⓒ	Ⓓ

PART 6

Strategy A

When you see sentences that begin with or contain the word *if*, ask yourself if they are conditional statements. Identify if the conditional sentence is a real or hypothetical situation. Then check to see that the correct form of the verb is used.

(A)   *If* the company *has* a large enough budget, it *will be able to expand* its market.

(B)   *If* they *had* an unlimited budget, our plans *would look* very different.

(C)   *If* the management *had added* more money to its advertising budget, we *could have reached* more markets.

In the examples above, all sentences begin with *if* and are conditional sentences. Sentence (A) relates to a potential *real* situation (real future possibility); Sentence (B) describes a *present hypothetical* situation (present unreal possibility); Sentence (C) describes a *past hypothetical* situation (past unreal possibility). Note the verb tenses in each sentence.

> Grammar Glossary **Conditionals (p113)**

Task A

Identify conditional sentences

Complete the sentences with the correct form of the verb. The sentences are identified as real or as present or past hypothetical.

1   If the city *identified* the source of the leaks, it (save) _would save_ the taxpayers millions of dollars. *Present Hypothetical*

2   If I (know) .... that e-commerce was going to be such a financial success, I *would have invested* my money in different companies. *Past Hypothetical*

3   If the connection *is* made correctly the first time, there (be) .... no need to do any rewiring. *Real*

4   If management *values* savings and efficiency, they (contact) .... us about our newest software programs. *Real*

5   The farm machinery (not rust) .... if the family *had invested* in repairs to the barn. *Past Hypothetical*

Strategy B

Look out for adjectives that end in -ed (or other past participle ending, -en, -t, etc.) and -ing. Make sure that the form is correct for the meaning of the sentence.

The meaning might be **cause** (-ing) or **effect** (-ed).

> The investors heard some *frightening* news about the stock market.
> The *frightened* investors took their money out of the stock market.

Frightening describes the news, which causes the investors' feeling.
Frightened describes how the investors feel, which is the effect of the news.

Participle adjectives can also describe something that is **in progress** (-ing) or **completed** (-ed).

> Watch out for the *falling* bricks. (The bricks are falling.)
> The sidewalk was covered with *fallen* bricks. (The bricks fell down before and now they are lying on the sidewalk.)

Participle adjectives with -ing can describe a person or thing that is **active**.
> *Working* parents are very busy. (The parents work)
> The sound of *dripping* water helped us discover the leak. (The water drips)

Grammar Glossary **Participles: -ed / -ing** (p115)

Task B

Identify participle adjectives

Underline the correct form of the adjective.

6 Artificial intelligence is extremely *interested/interesting* to me.

7 These offices are chilly because the *heated/heating* system isn't working well.

8 The computer scientist tries not to make his lectures *complicated/complicating*, but he isn't usually successful.

9 The constant hum of the machinery was so *annoyed/annoying* that the employees had a hard time concentrating on their work.

10 The *tired/tiring* mechanic came to fix the machine at the end of the day.

11 The foreman was *puzzled/puzzling* by the miners' reluctance to return to work.

12 If you could teach me to fix these recurring problems, your job would be much more *relaxed/relaxing*.

13 They complain that the *painted/painting* body of the car is often chipped during shipping.

14 Entering the harbor by tugboat, the *loaded/loading* freighter finally reached its destination.

15 The *speeded/speeding* traffic makes this a dangerous street to cross.

Review

Directions: Select the best answer to complete the text.

Questions 16–19 refer to the following email.

To: Barney Quinn
From: Marlene Dumas
Subject: Missing and broken goods

Barney,

Thank you for processing our order so quickly. Unfortunately some of the items we ordered did not arrive or were broken. You used RXZ Delivery. Maybe you don't know their reputation. If you had not used them, we _____ a complete shipment today.

16   (A) would
        (B) have
        (C) will have
        (D) would have had

We ordered four cartons of two-liter flasks (four flasks per carton). Two of the cartons have been lost and three flasks in one carton were broken.

We ordered two XL-430 microscopes. Both were damaged. In this case they were not packed carefully. If you _____ stronger cartons, this would not have happened.

17   (A) had used
        (B) had been used
        (C) will have used
        (D) would use

We ordered six 205z LCD monitors. Only one arrived, but fortunately it arrived in perfect condition.

The shipping company is investigating the _____ items. They have also made a note of the

18   (A) miss
        (B) misses
        (C) missed
        (D) missing

broken items so you can make an insurance claim.

I regret that this happened. I would appreciate it if you could pack carefully and send us replacements for the _____ goods using a reliable carrier.

19   (A) damage
        (B) damages
        (C) damaged
        (D) damaging

Sincerely yours,

Marlene

Reading

Part 6

16 Ⓐ Ⓑ Ⓒ Ⓓ
17 Ⓐ Ⓑ Ⓒ Ⓓ
18 Ⓐ Ⓑ Ⓒ Ⓓ
19 Ⓐ Ⓑ Ⓒ Ⓓ

PART 7

Use the questions and answers to focus on an action that is being taken for a specific reason. Read the questions and answer choices before you read the passage.

Ask yourself: *"What is happening and why?"*

Why was the notice written?
(A)   Because the number of accidents is low
(B)   Because the lists are outdated
(C)   Because everyone is supposed to lower the number of accidents
(D)   Because employees have forgotten the safety procedures

Notice

Each division is being asked to look carefully at its safety record and to take action to improve it. In the last five years, there have been only two accidents in our post-production department. While that sounds very good, we can do better. The accidents that did occur were machinery-related accidents that could have been prevented. As a result, I am asking all of you to create a detailed list of the steps taken before and after use of all machinery, in order to identify areas in which we can improve our safety procedures.

All the answer choices begin with the word *because*, but note that *because* does not appear in the notice.

Which answer choices can you eliminate? (A) is illogical; a low number of accidents is a good thing. (B) *Lists* are mentioned in the passage; however there is nothing said about them being out of date. (D) This isn't mentioned in the passage and so can be eliminated. Therefore the correct answer is (C).

Task A

Identify possible reasons

Cross out those answer choices that do NOT identify a possible reason.

1   The supervisor was fired.
   (A) The control room was left unlocked overnight.
   (B) He had been working for fifteen years.
   (C) The computer system failed five times in two weeks and no one was notified.
   (D) He decided to file a lawsuit for unlawful dismissal.

2   The first genetically modified corn was taken out of supermarkets.
   (A) As a result, the company went bankrupt.
   (B) It was developed by scientists in a New York laboratory.
   (C) Severe side effects were discovered.
   (D) The corn was very expensive.

3   They weren't able to maintain their on-line connection when the telephone rang.
   (A) They had an outdated system.
   (B) They omitted a step in the process.
   (C) They gave up and bought a cellular phone.
   (D) They called the help line to solve the problem.

4   The painter became ill and was rushed to the hospital.
   (A) She forgot her face mask at home and had painted without it.
   (B) The doctors said that within a few hours she would be fine.
   (C) A new type of paint was being used.
   (D) She hadn't cleaned her paintbrushes.

Strategy B

Read the questions, answer choices, and passage quickly to identify a planned action. Sometimes, but not always, the planned action will be indicated by the future tense.

> What will be the result of the report?
> (A) Restaurants will become cleaner.
> (B) More restaurants will open in the city.
> (C) More employees will work for the organization.
> (D) 70% of the restaurants will be closed.

According to our latest records, 30% of the restaurants in the greater metropolitan area have received a rating of 2.5 or lower on their health inspections. A passing score for our purposes is 2.75. The number of restaurants not passing inspection has increased 10% in the last 2 years.

This trend, coupled with the increasing number of new restaurants, indicates the necessity for increased vigilance to protect the health of restaurant diners. Therefore, we will be hiring and training an additional 20 inspectors for our staff. The hiring will be complete by June 30.

(C) is the correct answer. All of the answer choices include the future tense indicated by *will*. You can eliminate choices by comparing the verb tense in the answer choice with the tense in the passage. Answer choice (A) is not mentioned in the report. It may be what the organization hopes for, but it is not stated. The passage says that the number of restaurants has *already* increased. This is not a projection for the future. Therefore, answer choice (B) can be eliminated. The report indicates that 30% of the restaurants may be closed, not 70%. Therefore, eliminate answer choice (D). Answer choice (C), which is directly stated in the passage, is the planned action of the report.

Task B

Identify a planned action

Cross out those choices which can NOT be a planned action.

5   A manager is unhappy with worker efficiency.
   (A) He will write a report.
   (B) He received a good review.
   (C) He will arrange a plant visit.
   (D) He is developing an interview form.

6   An engineer can't identify the source of a leak.
   (A) The water is cold.
   (B) She will run a series of tests.
   (C) She will talk to the employees.
   (D) 15 gallons have been collected.

7   The company is unhappy with its information system.
   (A) They will investigate new potential providers.
   (B) The systems were installed five years ago.
   (C) The engineers tend to favor the current systems.
   (D) Modifications will be made.

8   Production has no inventory of its best-selling CD ROM.
   (A) It sells for $25.
   (B) Last year, over 25,000 units were sold.
   (C) An emergency print run is being scheduled.
   (D) It will be taken off the shelves.

9   *Best Supplies* has to replace its toner every month.
   (A) Too many copies are being made.
   (B) A counter will be installed on the machines.
   (C) Business is great.
   (D) The competition closed for the summer.

10   The water registers an unacceptable level of chemicals.
   (A) Swimmers will be warned.
   (B) Beaches will be closed.
   (C) Tourism will increase this summer.
   (D) The chemicals are not dangerous.

Strategy C

One of the questions in the double passage set may ask you to identify a person or an occupation. Read the questions and answer choices quickly. Look for questions about people and decide if you will need information from both passages to answer the question. These questions usually begin with *who*.

1 Who should have taken care of the car's problems?
   (A) An automobile mechanic
   (B) An electronic technician
   (C) A sales representative
   (D) A customer service representative

To:	Rav's Luxury Car Rental
From:	M. Johnson
Subject:	Problems with your car

Last weekend I rented a car from your agency. The car heater would not work; the radio only had one station; the windshield wipers were too slow to be effective; and lights inside the car would not turn off. Don't you have any mechanics to fix these problems? This is the last time I rent a car from you.

To:	M. Johnson
From:	Seymour Park
Subject:	Your Rav experience

Dear Mr. Johnson,

Let me apologize for the inconvenience you experienced last weekend. All of our cars are thoroughly checked before they are sent on the road. Our mechanics look over the brakes, motors, and steering. Our electrical technicians check heaters, radios, lights, and other electronically controlled equipment. Our service department made a mistake. I will have our customer service representative offer you a free rental car as our way of saying "We're sorry."

Sincerely,
Seymour Park
Manager, Rav's Luxury Car Rental

(B) is the correct answer. Seymour Park writes that electrical equipment is serviced by electrical technicians. (A) and (D) These occupations are mentioned, but they do not service malfunctioning electrical equipment. (C) This occupation is not mentioned.

Task C

Identify a person

Match the situations (11–15) with the people (A–E).

11 Our photocopy machine needs a regular maintenance program.

12 Your research could produce a device that could earn millions for the company.

13 The motors in the heating and cooling systems in our building should be serviced.

14 The scientists are looking for someone to help with their work in the laboratory.

15 We need someone to advise us on how to establish a computer network.

(A) Product development researcher

(B) Information technologist

(C) Mechanic

(D) Lab assistant

(E) Office machine service technician

Review

Directions: Read the schedule and the email and select the best answer for each question.

Questions 16–20 refer to the following schedule and email.

Southern Oil Expedition, July 1–10

Schedule for July 1

8:00 a.m.	Report to dock for security clearance.
9:00 a.m.	Embarkation
11:00 a.m.	Briefing in Lido Lounge
12:00 noon	Lunch
1:00 p.m.	Set sail
6:00 p.m.	Meet in Lido Lounge
7:00 p.m.	Dinner

Please note: changes may be made to the schedule at a later date.

To...	**Personnel on Oil Exploration expedition**
From...	**J. Banks, CEO**
Subject:	**Policy Change**

All personnel should be aware of the following policy changes which will take effect on the next exploration trip. There are several environmental groups which oppose our drilling in the Pacific and we have received threatening letters from them. The governments of the involved countries have confirmed their support of our projects, however safety is still our first priority. Therefore, we are tightening security at the time of pre-boarding and during the trip south.

All personnel should resubmit their paperwork by June 20 to the captain and arrive three hours earlier than originally scheduled on the day of departure. This will allow us to thoroughly check the ship and crew for anything unusual. We appreciate your help in this matter. You are a highly valued crew and we want to make sure that this trip goes off without incident.

16 Why is the crew being asked to show up early?

    (A) To be inspected
    (B) To store the drilling equipment
    (C) To meet the new crew members
    (D) To turn in their documentation

17 Who is opposed to the exploration?

    (A) The new crew
    (B) Environmentalists
    (C) The oil company
    (D) The host countries

18 What is the oil company doing in response to the threat?

    (A) Canceling the trip
    (B) Ignoring the threat
    (C) Tightening security
    (D) Resubmitting their proposals

19 Why has the company sent out the notice?

    (A) To scare away the environmentalists
    (B) To change the ship's personnel
    (C) To alert the crew of changes
    (D) To inform the governments of their plans

20 What time should personnel report to the dock?

    (A) 5:00 a.m.
    (B) 6:00 a.m.
    (C) 8:00 a.m.
    (D) 1:00 a.m.

Reading

Part 7				
16	Ⓐ	Ⓑ	Ⓒ	Ⓓ
17	Ⓐ	Ⓑ	Ⓒ	Ⓓ
18	Ⓐ	Ⓑ	Ⓒ	Ⓓ
19	Ⓐ	Ⓑ	Ⓒ	Ⓓ
20	Ⓐ	Ⓑ	Ⓒ	Ⓓ

Grammar Glossary

Adjectives: Descriptive Phrases

Descriptive adjectives describe a quality or a state of a noun. Several types of phrases can serve as adjectives.

Participle phrase
The manager *waiting by the door near the window* is ...

Prepositional phrase
The manager *by the desk near the window* is ...

Infinitive phrase
The only manager *to get a promotion* is ...

Adjectives: Determiners

A determiner is a word that is used with a noun to limit its meaning in some way. The following classes of words can be used as determiners:

Articles
the, a, an

A letter was put on *the* desk near *the* window.

Demonstrative adjectives
Single   *this that*
Plural   *these those*

This letter was addressed to the lawyer who was out of town.
Can you see *those* people over there?

Possessive adjectives
Pronouns   *my, one's, his, her, its, our, their*
Nouns   *Kim's, the manager's*

My office is next to the *President's* office.

Numerals
Cardinal   *one, two, three*
Ordinal   *first, second, third*

The *third* time you are late you will lose one day's pay.

Indefinite quantity
more, most, some, few, any

We stayed *most* of the night working on a few projects.

Adverbs: Date/Time/Sequence Markers

Date, time, and sequence markers are used to tell when an event occurred.

Date markers
on, by, since, from ... to, before

I'll meet you in Seoul *on* the fifteenth of August.
I should arrive in London *by* the 26th of this month.
We've been in Milan *since* September 23rd.
I'm going to be in Riyadh *from* April 9th *to* April 12th.
The report should be complete *before* the end of the week.

Time markers
before, after, when, since, as soon as, by the time that ...

Before I open the meeting I would like to thank Mr. Park for changing his plans.
He said he would deal with it *after* he had made a few urgent phone calls.
When the time is right we'll put in an offer – but not before.
A great deal has happened *since* the last meeting.
I'll get on with the main point *as soon as* we have heard the minutes from the shareholders meeting.
By the time that we arrive in Paris, the new program should be in place.

Sequence markers
first, first of all, to begin with
second, secondly, then, subsequently, later
finally, to conclude, in conclusion, in the end

First, I would like to talk about our new program. *Then* I will tell you about the effects of the take-over. *To conclude* I will address the challenges we face in the coming year.

Adverbs: Frequency Words

Adverbs of frequency are used to discuss how often an action or event takes place. Common adverbs of frequency are:

always, nearly always, often, usually, sometimes, occasionally, rarely, hardly ever, never

We *always* lock the office when we leave at night.
She *nearly always* brings her lunch to work.

Maria *often* eats her lunch in the park, with Yoshi.
The company *usually* allows customers to visit the
  factory.
Groups of school children *sometimes* visit the offices.
The management *occasionally* buys lunch for everyone.
They *rarely* spend more than $5.00 on each employee.
Ms. Tamura *hardly ever* drives to work; she usually
  walks.
Mr. Sanchez *never* arrives late to work.

Adverbs of frequency can also be used to discuss
regular occurrences. Common adverbs used for this
purpose are:

weekly, every day, every other day, yearly/annually

Our *weekly* meetings take place every Tuesday.
We have departmental meetings every day.
There are progress meetings *every other day*; on
  Monday, Wednesday and Friday.
Mr. Sung Park visits Seoul annually.

Cause and Effect

Cause and effect sentences indicate what happened
(the effect) and why it happend (the cause).
In a cause and effect sentence, either the cause or the
effect clause or phrase can begin the sentence:

(cause)   (effect)
The downturn in the economy has upset our expansion
plans.

(effect)   (cause)
Our expansion plans have been upset by the downturn in
the economy.

Some common words that introduce a clause of cause
or reason are:
*since, as, because, because of, due to, on account of,
out of, from*

(effect)   (cause)
We missed the start of the meeting, *on account of* us
being late.

Some common words that indicate an effect or result are:
*so that, so, as a result, therefore, consequently, thus,
resulted from, caused*

(cause)   (effect)
We were late for the conference and *as a result* we did
not hear the plenary.

Conditionals

Conditionals are used to describe hypothetical cause
and effect situations. There are three common types of
conditionals: real future possibility, present unreal, and
past unreal.

Real future possibility

If + present simple   *will* + base form
(*Hypothetical cause*)   (*possible effect*)

If I have time, I will finish the report tomorrow morning.
He will arrive at 9:00p.m. if he catches the 2:00p.m.
flight.

Present unreal possibility

If + simple past   would + base form
(*Hypothetical cause*)   (*possible effect*)

If I were promoted today, I would go to the London office.
I would send him a catalogue if I had his address.

Past unreal possibility

If + have + past participle   would + have + past
                              participle
(*Hypothetical cause*)   (*possible effect*)

This conditional is often used to express REGRET or
RELIEF about things that have never happened, which
could either have consequences in the present or had
consequences in the past.

Regret
  If she had worked harder, she would have passed the
  exam.
  We would have bought a bigger computer if we had had
  more money.

Relief
  We wouldn't have survived if the bank hadn't lent us
  the money.
  If I hadn't arrived late, I would never have met the new
  CEO.

Conditional: *should / would*

Should and *would* are sometimes referred to as the
conditional in sentences such as:

I should like to attend the conference in Saudi Arabia
next year.
I would join you in Penang for the meeting.

The condition *if* is implied in these structures.

I should like to attend the conference in Saudi Arabia
next year (if I can find the time).
I would join you in Penang for the meeting (if I could,
but I can't get away).

Gerunds and Infinitives

Gerunds

Gerunds are formed by adding *-ing* to the simple form of the verb. They are used in the following ways:

Subject nouns
Working for this company is very rewarding.

Object nouns
Most of our employees enjoy *working* here.

As the object of a preposition
Mr. Susumura is very happy *about transferring* to Washington DC.

Following the preposition *to*
We are looking forward *to meeting* you.

Many verbs and phrases are usually followed only by gerunds. These include:
admit, consider, deny, excuse, finish, involve, postpone, quit, regret, suggest, to keep on, there's no point in, to have difficulty.

Infinitives

Infinitives are formed by adding *to* to the base form of the verb. They are used in the following ways:

Following select verbs.
hope to, plan to, agree to, offer to, expect to, refuse to, need to

We *offered to redo* the proposal.

Following select verbs + noun/pronoun
tell someone to, invite someone to, allow someone to, warn someone to, would like someone to, need someone to, encourage someone to

I *would like you to back-up* your files before you turn off your computer.

Many verbs and phrases are **usually** followed only by infinitives. These include:
agree, arrange, ask, care, claim, consent, decide, demand

We *decided to outsource* all of our accounting functions.

Some verbs and phrases can be followed **only** by infinitives. These include:
begin, can't stand, continue, neglect, propose, try

We *tried to reach* you by phone this morning.

See a standard grammar text for extended lists of verbs to use with gerunds and infinitives.

Nouns: Count/Non-count

Count nouns refer to things that can be counted. They are expressed as either singular or plural.

computer/computers, employee/employees, office / offices, worker/workers, file/files, machine/machines, fax/faxes

Non-count nouns refer to things that cannot usually be counted.

machinery, food, water, love, work, training, homework, business, information, research, advice, news

Articles with count nouns

Singular count nouns take *a/an*.

I need *a* new computer.
The meeting is being held in *an* office in Sydney.

Plural count nouns take *some/any*.

Are there *any* workers in the dispatch office today?
I came to see if I could get *some* faxes sent out today.

Plural count nouns also take *many* and *a few*.

Our company doesn't have *many* employees.
There are only *a few* companies like ours in Thailand.

Articles with non-count nouns

Non-count nouns don't generally take *a/an*. Some of the articles used with non-count nouns are: *much, a little, a great deal of, a lot ... of* and *lots of*.

Unfortunately, we didn't get *much* work done today.
I'll ask him if he could spend *a little* time on this job.
We have *a great deal of* information on their activities.
He's going to need *a lot of* training for this work.
She requires *lots of* advice on this matter.

Nouns: Singular/Plural

Most nouns (words that name objects/places/people) are regular. The plural of regular nouns is formed by adding -s to the base form.

office/offices, employee/employees, file/files, desk/desks, car/cars

However, some English nouns are irregular. They have to be changed significantly to form the plural.

man/men, mouse/mice, tooth/teeth

See a standard grammar text for extended lists of irregular nouns.

Parallel Structures

Parallel structures are sentences containing two or more structures that share the same grammatical function, joined by an appropriate conjunction.

Parallel past simple

He *called* the waiter and *asked* for the check.

Parallel adjectives

She's *young* and *inexperienced*, but I think she'll work out.

Parallel infinitives

We have managed *to control* spending, *resist* excessive hiring, and *avoid* laying-off too many people.

Parallel gerunds

He enjoys *cycling*, *playing* tennis, and *walking* in his spare time.

Participles *-ed/-ing*

The present participle (*-ing*)

The present participle is formed by adding *-ing* to the base form of the verb. In addition to being used to form the progressive tense, the present participle functions as a gerund and as an adjective.

We *are buying* stock in the high-tech markets.
Buying stock can be very risky.
The *smiling* broker dealt with my request.

Past participle (*-ed*)

The past participle is formed by adding *-ed* to the base form of regular verbs.

We had *placed* the order too late.

Irregular verbs use a variety of endings.

The bank has *lent* us the money.
She will have *taught* the new employees the procedures by next week.

See a standard grammar text for extended lists of irregular verbs.

In addition to being used to form the perfect simple tenses (past, present and future), the past participle is used with *to be* to form the passive.

Our computers *were programmed* to shut down at midnight on Friday.

Parts of Speech

Nouns

Words that name people, objects and places.
man, John, desk, paper, office, hospital, Paris, Belgium

Verbs

Words that name actions, feelings and events.
walk, run, photocopy, negotiate, work, drive

Adjectives

Words that describe nouns.
a beautiful car, a lovely day, a wonderful report

Adverbs

Words that describe the action of verbs.
He ran quickly. They happily signed the contract.

Pronouns

Words that are used in the place of nouns.
he, she, it, they
his, her, its, their

Mrs. Jones works here. *She* works here.
The report is Mrs. Jones' work. *It* is *her* work.

Comparatives/Superlatives

Words that modify adjectives

fast/faster/the fastest
expensive/more expensive/the most expensive

Conjunctions

Words and phrases that join clauses

and, so, but, for, and yet, so that,
nevertheless, or, that, unless

Prepositions

Words and phrases that talk about time, location, possession, and direction

before this, *next to* the storeroom,
the leg *of* the chair, *to* the bank.

Articles

Words that indicate whether a noun is definite or indefinite
Definite (*the*)
   The man over there is my boss.
Indefinite (*a/an*)
   Would you give me *a* pencil, please?
Zero article
   __ Cats are not allowed at __ work.
Zero article is used with certain plural nouns or nouns that do not need an article.

Prefixes and Suffixes

Prefixes

Prefixes are groups of letters added to the beginning of base words that change the function or meaning of the word.

*dis*like, *de*centralize, *mis*manage, *super*market, *out*bid, *pro*-government, *inter*national, *post*script, *multi*cultural, *auto*biographical, *proto*type, *vice*-president, *semi*annual

Prefixes usually do not change the grammatical function of a word. Verbs remain verbs; nouns remain nouns, etc.

Suffixes

Suffixes are groups of letters added to the end of base words that change the function or meaning of the word.

Londo*ner*, wait*er*/wait*ress* (gender based), book*let*, brother*hood*, scholar*ship*, refin*ery*, grate*ful*, Malays*ian*, Yemen*i*, Japan*ese*, socia*lite*, socia*list*, idea*lism*, organi*zation*, centr*al*, sad*ness*, qual*ify*, worth*less*

Suffixes can change the grammatical function of a word. Verbs can become nouns or adjectives; nouns can become adjectives, etc.

See a standard grammar text for extended lists of prefixes and suffixes.

Prepositions: Objects

The prepositional object is the noun phrase following a preposition.

	Prep.	Prep. Object
His lateness only added	*to*	*the problem.*
Has the Board responded	*to*	*their demands?*
We really hope to build	*on*	*our success.*
Our creditors have asked	*for*	*help.*

Prepositional Phrases with *by*

Prepositional phrases with *by* indicate
  means (how?)
  time (when?)
  position (where?)
  agent (by whom?)

Means
  He arrived *by plane* from Brussels.
  (Explains how he arrived.)
  By signing this contract we have doubled our holdings.
  (Explains how have we doubled our holdings.)

Time
  By the time he arrived the work was finished.
  (Explains when the work was finished.)

Position
  She was *by the CEO* in the picture.
  (Explains where she was standing.)

Agent
  This report was written *by the Research Department.*
  (Explains who wrote the report.)

Prepositions of Location

These are generally used to describe the position of two or more objects, relative to each other.

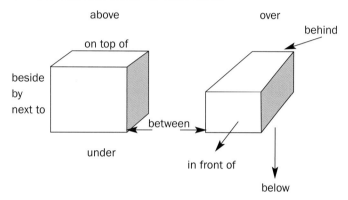

The visitors' parking lot is *between* the warehouse and the main office.
There's a pay phone *next to* the warehouse.
I'll meet you *by* the coke machine in front of the warehouse.
The employees' parking lot is two floors *below* the main office building.
There's a helicopter pad *on top of* the warehouse.
We can store this stuff *behind* the warehouse until we need it.
Is there any storage *in* the basement *under* the warehouse?
There's a sign *above* the warehouse.
We are worried about the planes passing *over* the main office building.
People usually smoke near the tables *beside* the main office building.
Our visitors park *in front of* the building.

Pronouns

Pronouns are used in place of nouns. There are three basic types of pronoun: subject pronouns, object pronouns and possessive pronouns. They can be singular or plural.

Subject pronouns
I, you, he, she, it we, you, they

  I read your report; *it* was very good

Object pronouns
me, you, him, her, it, us, you, them

They want to meet *us* on Friday morning.

Possessive pronouns
mine, yours, hers, his, its ours, yours, theirs

Is this your coffee or *hers*?

Subject and Verbs of a Sentence

All sentences in English must contain a subject and a verb.
In English the subject is usually the noun, pronoun or noun phrase that is the focus of the sentence. The predicate is the rest of the sentence, and contains the verb and object.

(*subject*)	(*predicate*)
Our latest acquisition	has been a real asset to our holdings.
Mario and Tina both	work in the Research and Development Department.

The subject determines the agreement of the sentence. (See Verb agreement)
In English the verb is part of the predicate and refers to the actions carried out by the subject.

	(*verb*)
Our latest acquisition	*has been* a real asset to our holdings.
Mario and Tina	*work* in the Research and Development Department.
They	*have been working* there for 2 years.

Synonyms

Synonyms are words or phrases that have similar meanings to other words.

place of work = *office, headquarters, agency, bureau*
hardworking = *assiduous, diligent, industrious*

Verbs: Active/Passive

There are two ways to express information in sentences that use transitive verbs (verbs that can have objects) – active and passive.

Active

In an active sentence the subject is responsible for the action; the object of the sentence is the recipient of the action. The subject (sometimes called the agent) is the focus in an active sentence.

(*subject/agent*)	(*active verb*)	(*object/recipient*)
The manager	purchased	the new software.
The Federal Reserve	lowered	the interest rate.

Passive

In a passive sentence the recipient of the action is the subject. The verb becomes passive by using the appropriate auxiliary verb and the past participle of the verb. The action is the focus in a passive sentence, not the agent.

(*recipient*)	(*passive verb*)	(*optional agent*)
The new software	was purchased	by the manager.
The interest rate	was lowered	by the Federal Reserve.

Verbs: Stative

Stative verbs are verbs that are normally not used in the progressive tense (see Verb Tenses). They are often verbs of emotion or verbs that refer to ideas that do not change:

Verbs of senses
  see, hear, feel, taste, smell
Verbs of emotion
  love, hate, like, differ, desire
Verbs of perception
  believe, know, understand, remember
Verbs of measurement
  cost, equal, measure, weigh
Verbs of relationship
  belong, contain, have, own

Correct	Incorrect
I *love* working here.	I *am loving* working here.
My opinion *differs* from yours.	My opinion *is differing* from yours.
I *believe* you are correct.	I *am believing* you are correct.
We *own* that office block	We *are owning* that office block.

Also we normally use *have* in a stative manner when it is being used to describe possession.

Correct	Incorrect
I *have* a cold.	I *am having* a cold.
She *has* a new car.	She *is having* a new car.

Verb Agreement

The subject/verb must always agree in number. A singular noun takes a singular verb form and a plural noun takes a plural verb form.

Singular Subject	Verb
Our chief accountant	*lives* about twenty miles from the office.
An MA with five years work experience	*is* needed for this position.

Plural Subject	Verb
Most of our employees	*live* in the suburbs.
An MA and five years work experience	*are* needed for this position.

The subject and the verb must always agree, even if separated.

Separated by preposition
  Most of the ideas put forward by your department *are* good.
  The diagram on page sixteen in this training handbook *is* very good.

Separated by clause
  A lot of the things that I really love *were* in that suitcase.
  The number of people who came late today *is* very high.

Gerunds always take a singular verb
  Training our employees *is* an important part of our program.
  Smoking in the workplace *is* not allowed.

Verb Tenses

There are three time frames in the English tense system: present, past and future.

There are two simple tenses – present and past. The future is expressed using combinations of *will/shall* and *going to*. These three tenses can be expressed as either: simple, progressive, perfect or perfect progressive.

Present time frame
Simple Present
  She *checks* her e-mail every morning.
Present Progressive
  She *is checking* her e-mail at the moment.
Present Perfect
  She *has* already *checked* her e-mail.
Present Perfect Progressive
  She *has been checking* her e-mail since 9:30 a.m.

Past time frame
Simple Past
  She *checked* her e-mail at 6:30 last night.
Past Progressive
  She *was checking* her e-mail when the alarm rang.
Past Perfect
  She *had checked* her e-mail before I arrived.
Past Perfect Progressive
  She *had been checking* her e-mail all morning and felt tired.

Future time frame
Future Simple
  She *will check* her e-mail when she comes in.
Future Progressive
  She *will be checking* her e-mail when we arrive.
Future Perfect
  She *will have checked* her e-mail by 10:30 a.m.
Future Perfect Progressive
  She *will have been checking* her e-mail for 2 hours by the time we arrive.

To discuss future events we can also use *going to*, the simple present and present progressive.

going to Future
  She *is going to check* her e-mail before she leaves.
going to be + *ing*
  She *is going to be checking* her e-mail when we arrive.
Simple Present
  My plane *leaves* Boston at 7:00, and arrives in Washington at 8:30.
Present Progressive
  I *am meeting* my new boss at 8:45 tomorrow.

Verbs + Prepositions

Verbs often form partnerships with prepositions, called phrasal verbs. Many of these partnerships are idiomatic. The combined verb + preposition may have a meaning that differs from the meaning of the verb alone. The meaning can often be worked out from the context:

  The presenter *enlarged* on the topic during question time.
  Will he *run for* President next year?

Verb + preposition partnerships can be separable or non-separable. The meaning of the phrasal verb often changes.

Separable
  The credit card company *called* him *up* about his debts.

Non-separable
  The government *has called up* reserve troops because of this emergency.

Word Families

Word families are groups of words that have a common base word. Most word families consist of noun, verb, adjective and adverb.

Noun	photograph	exclusion
Verb	to photograph	to exclude
Adjective	photographic	exclusive
Adverb	photographically	exclusively

Noun	Look at *the photographs* of the new product.
Verb	We need *to photograph* the damage to the shipment.
Adjective	Our insurers want us to get a *photographic* record.
Adverb	We'll keep the evidence *photographically*.

Noun	We need to maintain an *exclusion* area around our research area.
Verb	Our competitors were *excluded* from the invitation.
Adjective	We have a very *exclusive* clientele.
Adverb	We deal *exclusively* with the international community.